Geetie's
COOKBOOK

love food
geetie and
x

"Real progress cannot happen without the driving force of ideals. It is through the world of work, not just through law or politics, that we will make the good society"

Abraham Maslow

Geetie's COOKBOOK

Recipes from the kitchen of the DUKE OF CAMBRIDGE ORGANIC PUB

Geetie Singh & Sara Berg

Grub Street • London

For Mabel and Birchwood

Acknowledgements

My thanks and enormous gratitude to everyone who has encouraged and kept driving me onwards when I needed it. To Mabel for joining us. Sara Berg, the Duke's head chef for the past few years and who has tirelessly, with patience and humour, written and tested these recipes with me. Fiona Ward, Tascha Franklin, Dom Bailey, Gareth Hemsley and all the brigade at the Duke who, without, the Duke would not be what it is, you are the pub. Paul Whitby, my partner, friend, my sounding board, critic, and the wind beneath my wings! Mum and Geoff who have endlessly, at short notice, dropped what they been doing to help, babysit, type, read, edit and inspire. Anne Dolamore for pushing me when I needed it as well as all her hard work and all at Grub Street. Sukie Smith who understands the motivation and Louise Kamara the ethics. Pace Homer-Marsh, Caroline Bennett, Sam Wilds, Roger Mortlock, Anne Richardson, Charlotte Jarmen, Hardeep Singh Kholi, Matthew Clarke, Lester Wilson, Dom Gill and all who have invested in Sloeberry. Floyd Singh-Power, my friends in Gladestry, the people in Birchwood Hall who gave me the strength. The Soil Association, Charles Clover, Craig Sams, Tescopoly, Marine Conservation Society, Marine Stewardship Council, Joanna Blythman, Felicity Lawrence and Greenpeace for the wonderful resources of knowledge.

Published in 2010 by
Grub Street
4 Rainham Close
London
SW11 6SS
Email: food@grubstreet.co.uk
Web: www.grubstreet.co.uk

Text copyright © Geetie Singh 2010
Copyright this edition © Grub Street 2010
Principal photography by Tricia de Courcy Ling
Additional photography by Al Lapkovsky
Design by Kurtz_Design, London (www.kurtz.co.uk)

A CIP record for this title is available from the British Library

ISBN 978-1-906502-49-2

Printed and bound in India
Printed on paper from sustainable resources.

Contents

"Never doubt that a small group of committed citizens can change the world, indeed it's the only thing that ever has."

Margaret Mead (Anthropologist)

Introduction

Early Years at the Commune

Birchwood was, and still is, a Victorian mansion of splendour and from 1972 to 1986 it was home to me and the commune I grew up in. It was an idyllic existence which meant it was partly responsible for my lack of formal education.

During my childhood years there were usually between 10 and 15 adults and 5 to 10 kids living at Birchwood. We grew all our own fruit and vegetables and all ate together every evening, mostly with our homegrown or wild picked produce. The hour or so long dinner times were always full of lots of animated discussion and everything topical was analysed in exactly the same way we analysed our food. The adults took it in turn to cook, so on average once every 10 days, and the kids helped with chopping and table laying and rounding up the hordes from the 40 rooms when it was time to eat. You pretty much knew what was on the menu according to who was cooking, but some of the adults, especially the ones who did most of the veg growing were more adventurous. I think we ate everything that wasn't poisonous at Birchwood. I loved the salads, every variety of wild edible leaf and flower imaginable. We bought Fair Trade coffee from Oxfam which was pretty grim then so having a cup of Nescafé at my friends' houses was a guilty treat but I would never have bought the stuff; that would have been dancing with the devil as far as I was concerned.

Breakfast was eaten not as a group but when you needed it. As a kid you were used to coming down and finding a bemused stranger standing in the huge kitchen among the stores of everything bought in bulk and having to show them where stuff was. We mostly ate our homemade yoghurt (my mum's speciality) with muesli or homemade bread (Jock's speciality), always brown, which varied from heavenly to sometimes extremely heavy.

When I was really small and there were a lot of other children we used to have kids' tea. This was a riot of unkempt hippy tots who ate what we were given and enjoyed every mouthful! I remember eating Jemima the goat, who had died of natural causes – there were many vegetarians but it was wasteful not to eat her! We all sat there saying, 'yummy Jemima'. Not only did we eat her but Doreen wanted the skin for her floor so the hide was pegged out on the grass and scraped and dried. I wonder if she still has Jemima somewhere?

The most wonderful things to me were the vegetable garden and the orchards but the entire 8 acres of gardens were beautiful with terraces, woodlands with bluebells, walled rose gardens and a tennis court.

The orchard must have been about an acre and a half. It had apples – Cox, Bramley, and Russets – Conference pears (which I loved the hardness of, even when they were not ripe), damsons, Victoria plums, greengages and a giant walnut tree, which was also good for climbing. The vegetable garden was probably about half the size and provided potatoes, swede, runner beans, peas, broccoli, garlic, herbs, raspberries, strawberries, gooseberries, rhubarb and much, much more. It was also the site of an enormous Victorian greenhouse complete with a heating system fuelled by an oil stove in the back room. We didn't use the heating; you didn't

"I feel extremely lucky and privileged to have been brought up the way I have and as a result it's been very easy and obvious to me to run my adult life and my business how I do."

We tried hard to be self sufficient and wastage was not allowed. Everything got eaten and what couldn't be, got composted. If we ever had to buy in we bought from the local farms within walking distance from our house. If we used a normal shop for veg it was the greengrocer in town who also sourced from the local farms. This was entirely deliberate. We understood even then about food miles and chemical usage. They used to spray the crops around our lovely organic retreat using small aeroplanes and when they did we ran inside the house, shut all the windows and doors and hid. My mate and I discussed putting sugar in the fuel tank once but were far too good to do it. In retrospect, as long as the plane didn't crash with the pilot in it, it would have been a brilliant thing to do.

We grew far more than we could eat. Or maybe it was just that there was a limit to how many runner beans you could eat in a month! So preserving became essential and without a freezer – too expensive and too wasteful with energy – we turned to the traditional methods of pickling cucumbers and walnuts and preserving plums and apples. But we also salted. This involves buckets of salt and lots of patience, as does all food storage. I have such vivid memories of sitting on the top terrace in the summer heat looking out over the stunning view with mum and the other kids, topping, tailing and stringing the beans and laying them side by side in a bed of salt, covering them with another layer of salt and then adding the next batch of beans. When winter came and the memory of the beans had faded, we would rinse them thoroughly, and mum would make a wonderful bean curry.

really need to unless you wanted to grow exotic delicacies like pineapples or attempt to grow out of season. Inside were tanks to collect rain water, which was then stored at the temperature of the greenhouse to water the crops of tomatoes of all varieties, kumquats, aubergines, peppers, and cucumbers.

I used to go to that garden from a very young age and just feast. They called me 'the rabbit'; I would have had a salad over a pudding, and often did, any day. I loved raw broccoli and unripe fruit but I was never a huge strawberry or tomato fan. Later, when my Dad took me to the other world, to a very posh French restaurant, I remember ordering the salad with a stunning walnut oil which we had as a middle course, instead of a pudding, much to his embarrassment.

Beer and wine was also something we made ourselves although I think this was far more about saving money than ethics. Geoff (my step dad), the chief wine maker, would make wine out of anything and swore he could have made wine out of grannies' old boots! Elderflower wine was made of course, as was elderberry. Elderflower sparkle was a favourite of the kids and once we managed to pop the cork to land over the roof of the house, which at 60 foot was impressive. Picking that wild produce was a wonderful way of life. I guess for the adults it may have been a chore but as a child it was just fun (no doubt we had to be dragged away from some intense game).

> *"I was absolutely astounded at how these qualified, skilled chefs had no idea what season fruit or vegetables were in, were indifferent to where their meat was coming from, or what additives or chemicals the ingredients might be laced with."*

I feel extremely lucky and privileged to have been brought up the way I have and as a result it's been very easy and obvious to me to run my adult life and my business how I do. In my opinion what we eat and how we access that food is fundamental to our happiness. Food can make our lives completely miserable or it can be one of the most delightful and enhancing aspects of society. Our food industry is an inextricable part of our society. This may seem like an outlandish claim but you only have to read two wonderful books – Joanna Blythman's *The Food We Eat* or Felicity Lawrence's *Not On The Label* – to understand how we are destroying the planet and our society through food.

A plan is born

My childhood dream was to be a singer. I decided at the age of 14 that I was going to be the youngest opera singer on the Covent Garden stage. My school careers officer on the other hand thought I should be a secretary. However with a lot of help from my mum, my step father Geoff and my singing teacher Grayston Burgess, I somehow managed to get a place at Birmingham Conservatoire, part of Birmingham University at the age of 16. Sadly it was a pretty miserable experience; very competitive and academically driven and quite frankly my parents were right, I wasn't ready. I wanted to have fun. So I quit after a year and came to London.

I started working in restaurants. And I loved it. I loved the performance of service, the chaos in the kitchen, the hard physical work, the interesting people, the flexible hours and even the money. Though in those days I often didn't receive a wage at all, all your money came from tips, and I never

received a day's holiday or sick pay until I was in management.

But although I enjoyed the work, the industry as a whole seemed to be seriously lacking in any concept of provenance or ethic. I was absolutely astounded at how these qualified, skilled chefs had no idea what season fruit or vegetables were in, were indifferent to where their meat was coming from, or what additives or chemicals the ingredients might be laced with. Having worked in restaurants for a few years, I realised, out there, there was a market for people like me who wanted to know the provenance and ethics of the food they were eating in restaurants. I was striving for something more honest but at the same time more relaxed. And the uptight formality of the restaurant business just did not sit well with me.

It was 1993 when I came across The Eagle in Farringdon. This was it! Relaxed dining, simple food, ingredients led, simple wine lists and great beer all served in a classic pub atmosphere. What the Eagle had done, combining restaurant quality food and drink in a pub atmosphere, was a stroke of genius. It began the resurgence of bringing pubs back into the 21st century. Good food had been in pubs for years, but it was always the same kind of thing, steak and chips etc, in carpeted rooms with twee curtains. The Eagle took the bare building and the bare ingredients and served them up in a simple atmosphere. The simplest ideas are the best.

I was 23 years old and my plan was born. I wanted a 'gastro pub' as the Eagle's neighbour *The Guardian* had named it. But I wanted it to be ethical, sustainable, traceable and values driven. It had to be, very first and foremost an excellent gastro pub, but backed up by values inspired by my upbringing, Anita Roddick and the Soil Association.

In order to learn about sourcing sustainable organic ingredients I starting working in a wholefood shop. Some of the suppliers that we used there were the same ones we used in the commune; at the pub I still use them to this day. Whilst at the shop I was working in different restaurants and pubs to try and cover any areas of expertise where I felt I was lacking. Learning about wines in one, beer in another or cash systems on another. Many jobs at once.

I started writing business plans, but my poor education was finally catching up with me. I did some research at Mintel and the stats were there to back the plan up. It dawned on me that I might need a business partner. I started trying to recruit one, I went through a couple of people who didn't work out, and then I stumbled on an old childhood friend Esther Boulton. Having shown her the idea, and talked her through the plan she was on board. A year after that first meeting we opened the Duke of Cambridge.

That year before opening was probably the hardest of all my time in business. Esther made the leap and left her job as a museum curator and started working in the restaurant industry. While holding down 5 jobs between us, in our spare time we wrote the business plan, sitting side by side on the floor of my bedroom; with Esther writing and me gabbing on about my ideas it quickly came to fruition. When there are two of you, you drive each other forward; you have a responsibility to each other which means there is no escape into displacement activities. I had to save every penny I earned to pay for the expenses involved in the planning stage, investors to be dined, architects to be paid for, projects that didn't come off, books, business plans, accountants and lawyers.

I thought that raising the money would be the hardest part, but actually with an extremely strong business plan, with Mintel stats, and a superb design by Paul my boyfriend, getting the investment was pretty easy. You had to have total confidence in what you were doing, which of course is not always easy. Raising money for new business is selling ideas. I had to have an alter-ego, which didn't allow any of my uncertainties to show. Of course there were huge doubts, questioning yourself is essential, if you don't you are heading for a disaster. It turned out the really hard part was finding a site.

We searched high and low for a pub; most were tied to breweries which meant we wouldn't be able to serve our own beer and wine so they were out. Free houses were snapped up by more stable propositions, landlords weren't really keen to lend to a couple of women with a risky idea.

Then one Friday afternoon we spotted the for sale sign outside the Duke of Cambridge, it was going to auction the following Monday. All weekend we tried to find a buyer, tailored the business plan to the location and sat at the site counting foot fall, shopping bags, cars and anything that might give an indication that this was the site we were looking for.

On Monday, no buyer on board, we went to the auction, business plan in hand. We tried to watch the buyers bidding; they were so discreet it was almost impossible to spot them. When the Duke came on I was a bag of nerves. Only one person bid, we followed him out of the door gave him a copy of the plan and asked him to lease us the pub. He said he would be in contact.

A few weeks later, good as his word, he called and agreed to lease us the pub. Finally, my dream was beginning to look like a reality.

The work begins

The money was raised, we had £150k promised from private investors (including a substantial amount from a friend Lester Wilson and loans from family) and £100k promised from NatWest Bank. Before we approached NatWest we spent our time visiting banks that we felt sure wouldn't invest in us, for practice. Getting to grips with the figures wasn't easy, not surprisingly we were asked difficult questions on the forecasts. But honestly,

you can make them look as good or bad as you want. They were based from extremely kindly employers and friends who had been generous enough to share their private accounts with me and guesses of how my pub might work in comparison.

The landlord had agreed to do all the building work. It turned out he owned most of the street and the pub was the last domino in his run.

> *"Around 10pm, a month into the 3 month building project, a call came from the manager at NatWest. Apparently our loan had been turned down. She hadn't got authorisation for it and the deal was off."*

Business contracts were drawn up between Esther and me and investors. Negotiations began on the lease. Esther had an old friend from college, Jez, who was an architect who specialised in the pub trade, he was on board.

Work had begun on the pub, moving the toilets and all the stores to the basements, centralising a catering kitchen, and creating the bar and restaurant area while working with all the features that the building gave us, saving everything quirky like the old stable window and wall which was integrated into the restaurant. All the furniture, floor boards and wood were reclaimed; a lot of my life was spent scurrying around London looking for reclaimed sinks, doors, wood, bars etc. It was winter; our landlord kindly lent us a freezing room in the dormant upstairs flats for our office. There is an afternoon which is particularly ingrained in my memory from that time. While sitting at my make shift desk water started to pour down all over me. I ran upstairs to investigate and there was a builder pissing in the corner!

Around 10pm, a month into the 3 month building project, a call came from the manager at NatWest. Apparently our loan had been turned down. She hadn't got authorisation for it and the deal was off. The first big lesson, get it in writing. All the kitchen equipment was ordered, works had begun, and this was a huge shock which could leave us bankrupt before we had started. My father, Gurmukh Singh, who had been a successful entrepreneur and had given much of his time over the years advising community-based businesses like Last Days of the Raj and Camden Garden Centre, had been advising me from his house in France. He thought it important that we tell the landlord of the pub as he was doing all the works. The landlord was fantastic. He said he would continue working for one more week but if we hadn't raised the money by then he would have to pull out of the project for the foreseeable future. Firstly we found another bank, Barclays – certainly not ethical, but the Co-op had no business banker we could talk to so it was impossible to begin discussions, and Triados wouldn't deal with alcohol (a constant problem with ethical investors). The Barclays manager was just what we needed. He went through our accounts thoroughly and said we were trying to raise too much money. Though we would only need £50k from him, but without collateral, he wouldn't lend it to us. Having scoured through the figures again, we decided he was right. The rest of the week was spent trawling round anyone we could think of who might have some money they wanted to invest. Two days before our deadline we signed up two new investors we had found through 'networking'. I didn't know that I could network, but clearly I wasn't bad at it. We were up and running again.

We hired and drove lorries around the country looking for chunky second hand antique furniture in auctions and junk shops which I knew from my childhood. We would arrive back to the pub at one in the morning, Paul and Jez would meet us, and unload. The builders (who were working through the night) thought we were bonkers, couldn't see the style at all, but I knew exactly how it was going to look. We still have some of those original tables in the pub; one of them only cost a pound. I coined a phrase for our style, 'junkshop minimalism', or if trying to be more descriptive, 'ethical, functional, utilitarian, junkshop, minimalism'.

groups of people who we hoped would be forgiving as it was a cheap nosh up.

The avalanche of press began the day before we opened, a full page in the *Evening Standard*, talking about our ground-breaking organic pub. The press just didn't stop and for the first 2 years I must have been interviewed at least 4 times a week but still 10 years on I do an interview at least once a week.

We broke even after just four months. The Duke of Cambridge's rapid success took us all by surprise, but I was ready for it. I had learnt, mostly from bad managers how not to do it, and now was my chance to try it all out my way. I had installed a solid weekly accounting system of stock taking, gross profit margin targets, record keeping of all wastage etc. We had weekly meetings with teams at all levels where everything was discussed in a non-critical, forward-looking manner. This I learnt from my step father Geoff Petty, who is a much published author on teaching and creativity. Geoff taught me recruitment was key to management – if you got that right in the first place then everything else would follow. He taught me techniques and management philosophies that I have practiced ever since. He, along with the other people I turned to for advice, guided me through an extraordinary learning curve of managing so many different facets of this new world of business.

The Opening

On the 14th of December 1998 the world's first organic pub opened its doors. It was an hour late, finally opening at 1pm. I had roped in Paul, my brother and parents to help put the final coat of floor wax on and we were on our knees polishing away while patient customers waited outside looking rather perplexed. As we served the first customer, our first omission came to light; we had tills, programmed and ready but no change in them. My family's pockets were emptied while someone dashed up to the bank to get money for the float. That first lunch was a success, serving 20 people, which went down brilliantly well. We served all the food at half price for the first 5 days allowing us to make all our mistakes on these early

> *"We still have some of those original tables in the pub; one of them only cost a pound. I coined a phrase for our style, 'junkshop minimalism'."*

All the food was sourced from organic suppliers and we started the process of getting certification from the Soil Association. The problem was that there were hardly any restaurants going down this route, only a couple before us had done so. The certification process was laborious and badly designed for caterers. We were using a system for producers. The hours of people time it was taking

up was ridiculous. We had our first inspection, and when we received the report back I was shocked. It was a tirade of criticisms, no offer of solutions to the problems they were creating. I called the Soil Association, furious and told them to "sod off" saying that we had worked so bloody hard for this and they were offering no help with a useless system. They responded brilliantly. They set up a catering working group of which I became chair and over 2 years the new straight forward catering standards were born.

But I wanted to go far and beyond being organic. We were using Ecover cleaning products everywhere to start with but they were hopeless in the big commercial washing machines. So compromises were made while alternatives were looked for. I wanted soap without packaging in the loos, blocks of wonderful organic soap were in, but they dry up

and crack when in commercial situations for some reason. Liquid soap was resorted to, organic and produced in this country in refillable bottles. As soon as it was possible we signed up to a green electricity tariff and then with the best producer of this type of energy. All our office equipment was as green as it could be and recycling became part of our routine. Ten years on, recycling still is hard work and time consuming, with little help from the council who have only recently started to divert very small amounts of commercial waste from landfill. For example, we have to use separate companies to collect the compost, glass and other recyclables. The amount of space needed to store for weekly collections is huge and the time moving it all up and down from the basement wasteful. I am hopeful this will change as government legislation becomes tighter but without financial incentive at present there isn't much hope.

"The Duke of Cambridge has continued to be phenomenally successful, seeing its sales rise every year. It has hosted some magnificent events from the Soil Association, Friends of the Earth and the Green Party."

Gurmukh encouraged us to create a board of directors; in this we included him, another investor Matthew Clark, a solicitor and later Dom Gill joined us. The support, advice and contacts of this team were invaluable. Matt Clark has remained on the board all these years, he has been an amazing source of acumen, knowledge and understanding in tough times. It is still incredibly useful to have someone who has a vested interest and a passion for the business to talk to about ideas and issues.

Fish was clearly an issue. We tried to use small suppliers who were buying from sustainable methods, but what did this really mean? There was no information out there. We linked up with the Marine Conservation Society and laboriously put together a fish purchasing policy. This was the first restaurant fish purchasing policy in the country approved by them. We asked our suppliers to commit to the rules included in the policy and they signed up to it. But it became clear that as they were buying from Billingsgate Fish Market they had no idea where and how the fish was being caught. We started to look for alternative suppliers and came across Ben Woodcraft of Ben's Fish. He was an ex-fisherman who had set up a supply chain between restaurants and small sustainable fishing boats. Ben and I had animated conversations about all the problems with stock levels and methods and a loyal relationship was born. We still mostly use Ben, but we have a couple of other suppliers too: the Hastings certified Marine Stewardship Council fishery and Chris Bean, a day boat family team in Cornwall.

I was very clear from the start that the business should be driven by values rather than profit. For example, it was crucial that the whole team were given fair pay and terms of employment. I had contracts and job descriptions drawn up, with holiday pay for all. I gave a minimum wage of £6 per hour plus tips. This, you must remember, was at a time when none of this was law; in post Thatcher Britain, there was no minimum wage, holiday or sick pay and you certainly never got any kind of contract in catering. If you wanted good staff you had to pay for it. But, tragically, after a couple of months it became clear that £6 per hour was not affordable and we had to drop it down to £5. The team were brilliant about it, their tips were excellent so they were completely understanding. My philosophy was paying off already.

As the years have progressed the values haven't changed much. They have been able to expand as the market has begun to have a dramatically bigger sector of businesses that tie in with what we were trying to do. In the early days the supply chain was extremely limiting, meaning that choice was small. For example, in the very beginning, although we strived to buy only British vegetables, our range of vegetable buying had to extend to Europe. This seems outrageous now, as we predominantly buy from the Home Counties, but in order to stick to our certified status we had no choice as the supply chain just wasn't there. By 2005 it was possible only to buy UK produce other than lemons and sometimes garlic. Other organic restaurants were opening and closing saying it wasn't possible to have access to ingredients or at affordable prices, including, famously, Antony Worrall Thompson, so what I was managing to do felt ground breaking. At the same time I was keeping our prices absolutely competitive.

In the first few years, trying to implement all the values I'd dreamed of felt out of reach. It began to depress me. One evening my mum went to hear Anita Roddick talk. Afterwards she bought Anita's book at her signing, and while doing so mum told her about my business and asked her if I could contact her. She gave mum her PA's phone number and said I should get in touch.

Delighted, I did so immediately and was invited to meet with Anita for half an hour. Questions prepared, arriving at her headquarters we were

Judging the Soil Association Food Awards

ushered into her light filled office stuffed with colour and the activities of the Body Shop. She was a buzzing creature, quite hard to keep up with; you could see clearly how she had driven this phenomenal company forward. I explained that I had read her book, *Business as Unusual* and felt overwhelmed by what I wanted to achieve and how far I had to go. She laughed and pointed out that that book had been written only recently and that I should go back to her first book to understand how long it had taken her to get this far. She also tried hard to persuade us that expansion was not the way forward, that as a small local business you could have a sustained and effective impact by utilising the community – I was fairly dismissive of this at the time; generally I was good at taking advice, but this was one I ignored. Anita was inspiring, she gave me confidence that what I was doing was worthwhile, she also made me understand that you have to know what your limitations are as a business and work within them.

Expansion seemed inevitable. 'Brand and expand' was the dot.com boom motto and we were in the middle of it. The business had been amazingly successful so far. 'Brand and expand' felt wrong but it was also impossible to fight. Anita was the one wise voice saying no to expansion, but with her massive global business behind her, it appeared to me unconvincing. So expansion went ahead. We opened two more pubs in three years. The second, The Crown, was hugely successful but the third, the Pelican, not. We sold the Pelican eighteen months after opening. The sound advice of the board of directors saved us from bankruptcy. They encouraged us not to hang onto something that wasn't going to work for us. So many small restaurants that expanded during that period went bankrupt; we have our board and shareholders to thank for ensuring that we got out before it was too late. We sold The Crown in 2003, which enabled us to raise the money needed to buy Esther out of the business. Esther had got together with Jez the architect and she was pregnant. It felt the right time for both of us for her to move on from our partnership.

Now 11 years on from those first backbreaking and thrilling months and years of start up, the Duke of

Cambridge has continued to be phenomenally successful, seeing its sales rise every year. It has hosted some magnificent events from the Soil Association, Friends of the Earth and Green Party not to mention lunch for Tony Blair and family. The people I have met from WWF, Greenpeace, Friends of the Earth, *The Guardian*, City University and Sustain who have held meetings at the pub discussing important policy changing issues, have enriched me.

The Awards that have poured in have been overwhelming, from *Time Out,* Asian Woman of Achievement, *The Observer* and Business in the Community, to name just a few. The press accolades have been outstanding. But most of all we have led the way, pioneering green catering business into the 21st century and I have loved every minute of it. I am deeply proud of the work I have done with the team at the pub, our farmers, brewers, fishers and all our suppliers. In May 2009 I was honoured with an MBE.

We have tried to work with farmers as close to London as possible. Nearly all of our meat has always come from the Home Counties with the odd exception. One of these was a pork farmer from Devon. We had met him at an event we held at the Duke to try and link up with farmers from

> *"Achieving Marine Stewardship Certification in the summer of 2008 meant the complicated task of finding supply chains."*

the London Farmers Markets. We invited them to the pub to talk about what they might be able to supply to us when they were delivering in town so we could tap into existing journeys and also buy unsold vegetables from slow days in the markets. This pork farmer called us a few weeks later and said he wasn't going to survive if he couldn't sell another half pig a week. We agreed only to buy the half pig but as he was based in Devon, we would only accept delivery when he was coming to London for the farmers markets deliveries anyway. He has turned his farm and his wonderful meat into a successful business, though sadly due to the

price rises in feed, in 2008 he has had to drop being organically certified, so we can no longer buy off him.

Achieving Marine Stewardship Certification in the summer of 2008 meant the complicated task of finding supply chains. We only buy the MSC fish that is local to the UK so we end up with a pretty small range that isn't available through our existing suppliers. Through one of our farmers, Todd from Food for Thought, we hit on the brilliant idea of the Hastings Fishery delivering to him, our main meat farmer, who is also in Hastings and in turn his bringing all the stock to us. Fantastically efficient delivery systems!

Work outside the Duke

We have settled into a smooth rhythm with a brilliantly dedicated and enthusiastic team enabling us to work with schools. It all began with Islington Council's contract for school meals being up for renewal. A group of parents got together to try and ensure that the next contract was going to be an improvement on the past dreadful offerings. My agenda was to try to get the council to bring the whole thing in house again and make it sustainable and healthy. I didn't succeed but we did manage to get them to increase the spend per head, take on a better catering contract and set up a system for monitoring it which included parents. In the meantime a local primary school decided to pull out all together and take their kitchen in house and we offered to help. The cooks started by joining us at the Duke to see the possibilities of what can be prepared from scratch, on what scale and the time it takes. Then we started working with the cooks at the school analysing their recipes, costings, and linking them up to new suppliers. A year later they have a successful kitchen.

In July 2008 we worked with a secondary school. Taking 100 girls over 2 days, we trained them to cook and serve lunch for the other 250 girls in the school. It was enormously moving helping the

pupils; some of them were amazingly interested and inspiring in the kitchen and on the floor. Some were hard work and demanding, but the end result was empowering for them and for us. The teachers were deeply impressed with the girls effort and of the success of the event.

Natascha Franklyn, the sous chef at the pub, has an enormous talent for this work and is presently helping a nursery to recruit a team to create their entire menu from home-cooked, organic, local and sustainable sources.

The Soil Association catering standards committee turned out to be just the first of the fascinating boards and committees I have been invited to join, from London Remade to the Government's Women's Enterprise Committee. Presently I am a member of the Soil Association Council, the London Food Board, the Council of Food Policy Advisors (DEFRA) and a board member of the People Tree Foundation. I am so thrilled that my philosophies that were so scorned when I first started working in catering 20 years ago are now taken so amazingly seriously by so many people and are being integrated into everyday life.

From a food point of view I have watched society change from one extreme to the other and now we

> *"Only half of the food consumed in the UK today is produced here and we are now slowly realising that relying on imported food puts our own food security at risk."*

are heading back again. It's come from grass roots to the mainstream and our political leaders are taking heed. They will only listen to us if they think it's something they can win votes on. Be pushy and make change. Let all businesses put into practice how they would like to see their planet, farms, children, and lives be lived.

So let's shout about what we want for our food culture.

Our changing food culture

'Live life as if you were to die tomorrow, farm as if you were to live forever.' Adapted from a Mahatma Gandhi quote.

Only half of the food consumed in the UK today is produced here and we are now slowly realising that relying on imported food puts our own food security at risk.

I was born in 1969 in London and moved to Herefordshire in 1972. As a young country girl I watched seasonal and local food rapidly and dramatically decline. I remember the apple orchards of my childhood being ripped out. I watched as Herefordshire and Worcestershire, which had been top fruit-growing country for decades, lose most of its diverse range of ancient fruits and with it an age-old landscape.

'In the 1970's UK fruit producers were subsidised to grub out apple trees. Half of Britain's apple orchards disappeared. Imports from Chile, South Africa, the USA, New Zealand and Europe, often coated in preservative fungicides such as Captan or diphnylamine, filled the gap.' The Little Book Of Food, *Craig Sams.*

The gaps that we have created in agriculture and the skills being lost as a result are becoming alarmingly apparent. I'm not suggesting that we go back hundreds of years and have virtually no imported foods, but we should be self sufficient in our seasonal staples. We should prepare for a fuel crisis and be able to provide for ourselves. We need a food transport system that doesn't rely on huge centralised depots, we need localised abattoirs and small efficient local processing plants.

Our regional, local and homemade food began to decline as technology simplified food production, making it less time and manpower intensive. But how did our food culture change in such a relatively short period of time? Through a combination of big business and lack of political guidance. Supporters of intensive farming, supermarkets and food manufacturing have looked after their own interests with unforgivable short sightedness. Governments, who are after all employed by us to take care of our society, have positively encouraged this mutation of our food industry in the name of 'high yields and increased profits' but without apparent thought for the environment, community and farming industry. The food crisis in this country, with the likes of BSE and foot and mouth has cost us, the tax payer, unnecessarily, tens of billions of pounds.

Cookery in schools was dropped from the curriculum almost 40 years ago, deemed outdated and too expensive. As a result our domestic cooking skills have vanished, as has our knowledge of the seasons, vegetables, meat, their cuts and fish species. In homes with both adults working ready meals are sold as a solution but these are fat, salt and sugar saturated. With this huge cultural change have come hyperactivity, heart disease, diabetes and obesity. The cost to the health service is and will be far beyond what we can afford. The cost to people's lives is unquantifiable.

In the UK nearly a quarter of adults and 10% of children are classed as obese. Globally it is estimated that there are a billion overweight people while 800 million are chronically hungry due to poverty or lack of access to food. Food Matters, Cabinet Office.

But all is not doom and gloom. A small but significant revolution has begun. A most marvellous food revolution. Driven by independently minded passionate people, we are all rediscovering local, artisan and seasonal food. Traditional cheese making is having a resurgence, rare breeds of animals reared for taste and texture – not just yield – are being rescued from the brink of extinction, and our orchards are being replanted with our old majestic varieties of apples, pears and cherries. Pubs, restaurants and shops are opening in every corner of the country serving these fantastic ingredients with the skills that would make any French town green with envy. We can proudly proclaim, this century, that London's eateries outshine those of Paris hands down.

Organic food and farming

'There's no use dedicating billions of dollars to stimulate failed chemical-based farming schemes or to prop up industrial livestock systems that pollute air and water, excessively concentrate animals and animal waste, and require massive transport of crops that are never recycled back to their fields of origin. It's time to close the loops that depend on fossil fuels, and invest in systems where natural cycles create sustainable outcomes.' Greg Bowman, communications manager at the Rodale Institute in America, 2009.

The pioneer and campaigner Lady Eve Balfour, who began farming in the 1920s, recognised that the changes in the farming industry were looking only at short term gains. She saw the need for an alternative lobby to try to protect the soil, the countryside and the environment and by the creation of the Soil Association in 1946 the organic movement was born. It was as if she presaged the 1947 Agricultural Act which encouraged the use of chemical aids by subsidising fertilisers which ICI, having worked out how to turn its excess chemicals from the Second World War for use as agrichemicals, had lobbied the government for.

The organic movement has now become a massive business with a turnover that tops £20 billion world-wide. This crusade has been driven by the people. With each industrialised food horror outbreak, sales of organic food rocket. There has been little help from the government to fund or subsidise this life-preserving way of farming because the big business that opposes it has a more powerful lobby than those for it. Yet year on year it outstrips its predicted growth due to you, the customer proving with your spending power, that this is the way you would like to see your land and wildlife conserved. People understand it is a safer way to eat food they can trust.

'Biodiverse, local, organic systems produce more food and higher farm incomes while also reducing water use and the risks of crop failure due to climate change. Increasing the biodiversity of farming systems can reduce contribution to drought.' Vandana Shiva, physicist and a leader of the International Forum on Globalisation.

Introduction

'Organic farming, I am sure, will feed the world. I am also sure that unless organic farming re-expands, the human component of the world will eventually shrink. And, if climate change is not curbed, there will be no biosphere as we now know it, let alone food as we now have it.' Dr Tewolde Berhan, Director General of Ethiopia's Environmental Protection Authority.

Organic farmers recognise that our health is directly connected to the food we eat and aim to produce that food from a balanced living soil. They place strong emphasis on protecting the environment. They use crop rotations to make the soil more fertile. For example, a farmer might graze sheep on a field one year, then plant wheat the next and so on. Strict regulations, known as standards, define what they can and can't do. They can't grow genetically modified crops and can only use – as a last resort – seven of the hundreds of pesticides available to farmers (the Soil Association, however, only allow four of these). Parasite problems in farm animals are controlled through regularly moving the animals to fresh pasture and other preventative methods, rather than routinely dosing the animals with drugs.

The word organic is defined by law. Any food labelled organic must meet a strict set of standards.

Why are more people choosing organic?

1. Better for your planet
Over 20% of the UK's greenhouse gas emissions come from food and farming today. Nitrogen fertiliser manufacturing is the worst offender. To produce just one tonne takes one tonne of oil, seven tonnes of greenhouse gases and one hundred tonnes of water. Organic farmers work with nature to feed the soil and control pests. By choosing organic, local and seasonal – we can significantly reduce our carbon footprint.

2. Your well-being
No food has higher amounts of beneficial minerals, essential amino acids and vitamins than organic food. Organic food avoids pesticides and all controversial additives including aspartame, tartrazine, MSG and hydrogenated fats. Organic food contains higher levels of vitamin C and minerals like calcium, magnesium, iron and chromium as well as cancer-fighting antioxidants and Omega 3. Organic milk for example, is on average 68% higher in Omega 3 essential fatty acids.

3. Kind to animals
Animal welfare is at the heart of organic systems. Soil Association standards for meat and animal products rigorously protect all aspects of animal wellbeing – from rearing, feeding and shelter, to transportation and slaughter. Organic animals are free to pursue natural behaviour because they have plenty of outside space to thrive and grow, and are not routinely drugged with antibiotics. Organic standards prohibit cruelty and guarantee truly free-range lives for farm animals.

Yes, that's right. Many shoppers don't realise that organic products are also free range. Eggs and meat with the Soil Association symbol have been reared to the highest level of free-range standards. Birds are looked after in smaller flocks, spend more of their lives roaming outside on fresh grass and have more space in their houses.

4. Encourages wildlife
The UK Government's own advisors found that plant, insect and bird life is up to 50% greater on organic farms. Organic farming relies on wildlife to help control natural pests, so wide field edges are left uncultivated for bugs, birds and bees to flourish. They are also not sprayed away by the fertilisers, chemicals and pesticides routinely used on non-organic farms.

5. GM free
Genetically modified (GM) crops and ingredients are banned under organic standards. Shoppers wanting to avoid GM products may be surprised to know that over a million tonnes of GM crops are imported each year to feed non-organic livestock, which in turn supply our supermarkets with pork, bacon, milk, cheese and other dairy products.

Source: Soil Association (web site)

Introduction

Seasonal and local

It has been said that the blossoming of organic, local and home-grown food is only for the wealthy. But all movements start somewhere. And they spread. And yes it's most likely that the affluent have the time and money to 'indulge' in this coveted 'life style' of real food, but a revolution is in full swing. Go to any part of the UK now and there is likely to be a farmers', weekly or Women's Institute market selling local foods. They are open to anyone, and everyone is using them.

Let's celebrate the origins of 'local and seasonal' food. It has been in our society since time began, and you can be sure it was the worker who knew about how to grow, forage and harvest, not the landed gentry. If this was just a passing phase for the rich it would be limited to the grand food halls, but the supermarkets are shouting 'me too', which is deeply ironic as they are for a large part responsible for the crisis in farming today. They

> *"This may seem frustratingly limiting at first glance but lack of choice can be fun and once you are in tune with the seasons, it is hugely fulfilling as you experiment with what's available."*

have created distribution systems that will never allow them to work in any relevant quantities with local farms. And major food producers are trying to catch up too; Heinz is just one of the conglomerates who saw this marketing potential in 2007 by launching a Farmers' Market brand of tinned soup. They were criticized by both the public and food campaigners as the soup has nothing to do with farmers' markets but the Advertising Standards Authority judged their ads were not misleading.

'40% more birds were found in a three-year UK study of 44 organic farms, twice as many butterflies and five times as many wild plants.' The Little Book of Food, *Craig Sams.*

At present half of the food produced is thrown away – much of it by shops, restaurants and hotels, but much by us at home. "Sell by" and "Use by" dates absolve us from making our own sensible judgements, but will have been the cause of much of this waste.

Clearly we can pay more, for less food, thereby reducing the energy used in production, reducing waste, landfill and pollution. Quality food will help look after our society and health, therefore saving on our health service and the waste it sends to landfill and incinerators. The present style of food industry is cheap for the supermarkets who don't have to carry the costs of the consequences, but it's expensive for YOU. And you do pay, in TAX.

Seasonal

The energy used to grow produce in heated greenhouses accounts for 26% of British agriculture's energy use, and refrigeration 3.5%. The most efficient way to produce fruit and vegetables, is in a field close to where they will be consumed, in season, in the UK. If you are buying out of season you are endorsing either heating, chilling or long distance transport. So unfortunately local cannot just be local-for-locals-sake when it comes to greenhouse gas (GHG) emissions.

It doesn't help that people have lost the knowledge of what's in season. Most people know strawberries in the summer or asparagus in the spring. Try this out on friends though: who knows when potatoes are in season or red peppers, aubergines or cauliflower? You will be amazed, people just don't know anymore, and that's true of professional chefs too! The beauty of shopping for seasonal ingredients, is that the weather and availability dictates what you can cook. This may seem frustratingly limiting at first glance but lack of choice can be fun and once you are in tune with the seasons, it is hugely fulfilling as you experiment with what's available. Celeriac and Jerusalem artichokes in winter, fresh borlotti beans and globe artichokes in summer. And the seasons are often

short, so it's a matter of bingeing while the ingredients are there or learning to preserve in ways that allow you to enjoy them in the sparse season. In fact I think we now have too much choice. I long for broad beans all year; when they first arrive they are heavenly but by the end of the season I am done with them till next year. If we eat only seasonally we become more adventurous with our cooking, we learn how to use swede, beetroot tops or turnips. We learn about eating young broad beans in their pod, then podded and at the end of the season peeling off their skins to reveal the tender bud within. We learn to use pulses early in the year when there is a dearth of vegetables.

Food needs the sun to ripen it. Tomatoes that have been allowed to ripen on the stem under the sun will be the most delicious fruit that will explode with flavour in your mouth. Try one mid-winter, either transported or grown in a heated greenhouse; if you're lucky it might taste of tomato, at worse it will be completely tasteless. Brussels sprouts are at their best after the first frost; as the earth changes so does the plant. Eating seasonally means ingredients are so much tastier that they will speak for themselves.

And seasonality doesn't just apply to fruit and veg. Fish have breeding seasons and so does meat, which, if adhered to, would impact on dairy, cheese and eggs. Meat and milk in the summer taste much better when the cattle are grazing on fresh grass and if you allow animals to breed in their natural seasons they require less energy from indoor heating systems and can rely on natural food; it makes a lot of sense if you think about it. The game season is in the autumn and winter months when the young have grown and before nesting has begun. Fish seasons are more complex but equally crucial. (See fish chart page 156)

Local
'Small farms produce more food per hectare or acre than large farms; they just do it with more people and lower chemical inputs.' The Little Book of Food, *Craig Sams.*

When an area is served by local shops rather than supermarkets, more jobs are maintained and profit is distributed locally rather than lining the pockets of those elsewhere. One huge benefit that is often forgotten in the desire for supposed 'convenience'

> *"Using an animal from nose to tail needs to become part of our lives once again. At the Duke we order whole animals and use everything."*

is the community. When small independent shops are the backbone of an area, people get to know each other, the shop keepers and the community bond with one another. When a community knows itself it looks after itself; it develops common purpose. Huge supermarkets are designed around cars; at one stage Tesco was insisting that the word 'local shop' could be defined by a half hour car journey. In the countryside that could take the whole day on foot!

If food is local it is likely to be fresher, taste better, be better for the environment, the economy and society. Buying from your local farm shop or farmers' market, butcher or green grocer, if you are lucky enough to have one, is probably the best way to get local food, especially outside cities. But try your local box scheme if these options really aren't available to you. It's extremely important to put pressure on your local shop to buy local and organic ingredients, they ignore you at their peril.

Cheap meat

'Large-scale industrial livestock production is immensely environmentally destructive and polluting. If those who practised it had to meet the full cost of their emissions and their waste, the conomic model would not work... The question is not should we pay more – but can we afford at all a system that threatens to leave us without a sustainable food production base just as climate change makes local British farming more vital than ever?' Felicity Lawrence, The Guardian, *29 January 2009.*

Much of our meat production systems are environmentally unsound (and horrifically cruel). The methane that livestock release accounts for a shocking third of GHG emissions in farming. Land is used to grow crops to feed the livestock. If the land was used instead for crops to feed us the energy reduction would be quantifiable. Pigs and chickens were once fed on kitchen waste, commercial or not, but due to the BSE outbreak feed now tends to be imported soya protein.

But, don't think for a moment that I am advocating we all become vegetarians. Land can act as a 'carbon sink' absorbing GHG. As there is plenty of land in the UK which is not suitable for crops – hills, wet lands and national parks, leaving livestock on these areas would maintain both the landscape and the carbon sinks. These are ideal spaces to be producing meat as a delicacy. Breading animals out of season in heated sheds is obviously disastrously bad news from an energy point of view. There is no reason why most livestock can't live without the need for alternative food sources other than that which well maintained fields can provide. They take longer to raise, and need more space, but this is just an added plus to their welfare and their flavour.

Eating a lot less meat and treating it as a delicacy is one sure way to reduce our environmental foot print. I have met many people near my house in Wales who talk of their childhoods, when they kept a pig for their family's annual meat consumption. They bought a piglet, fattened it up on kitchen scraps over the year till it was ready for slaughter. Every bit of that beast was used, drying, sausage making, scratchings, smoking and salting.

Using an animal from nose to tail needs to become part of our lives once again. At the Duke we order whole animals and use everything. This means we freeze or hang so we have enough for a whole roast of the same cuts. It also means that the pig's head, the neck, shoulder, trotters are all turned into delicious food of one sort or another.

Supermarkets have demanded cheaper and cheaper meat; offering deals on meat that can't but result in horrific conditions for animals. Most people who eat this "knock-down price" meat have no idea what they are endorsing. Industrialised animal farming has become cruel and dangerous causing horrors like BSE (mad cow disease), polluting us with hormones, while lowering human tolerance to antibiotics with their excessive use.

Introduction

It seems to me that BSE and cases of Creutzfeldt Jakob Disease were caused by practices that included deliberately feeding vegetarian animals with 'high protein' feed of dead carcasses and chicken faeces. I have asked farmers if they knew that this government-approved feed was made from animal remains and they all say they had no idea, 'it was obviously a bloody stupid thing to do' in the words of one. Because of this atrocity, stringent and otherwise unnecessary health and safety laws have been introduced. One consequence of this is that I cannot give the organic vegetable waste from the restaurant to the local city farm, or create a compost heap in my local eco-centre, because I might accidentally contaminate it with a bit of meat. My vegetable waste is therefore professionally composted. Because of the risk that an animal might come in contact with it, it has to be heat treated. One example of profit driven, industrialised, officially approved stupidity that is costing the earth. Quite literally.

> "Our oceans and our fish stocks are in immense danger. Yet this issue is overlooked simply because we can't see what's happening, so don't challenge it."

The hidden cost of cheap food

- Industrialised farming uses fertilisers and herbicides, growing crops intensively without letting the land rest. This destroys the soil's own nutrients and fertility and pollutes our rivers.

- Crops that are grown faster are weaker, and therefore more susceptible to insect damage. Insecticides used to control those insects not only have the ability to pollute the rivers; they also indiscriminately wipe out most insects which are bird food, and pollinators.

- Animals reared in conditions that are unhealthy and unnatural are more susceptible to disease, so are routinely given antibiotics. Doses have to be increased as resistance builds up. These antibiotics enter humans, in turn diminishing our response to antibiotics and those same antibiotics enter our water systems.

'Tesco says it works with suppliers to keep pesticide residues in fruit and vegetables to a minimum. Yet Government data shows that the company made no overall reduction in the level of pesticide residues in its food between 1998 and 2002. Hormone disrupting pesticides above legal limits have also been found in Tesco fruit and vegetables in 2004 and 2005. As well as posing a threat to human health, pesticide use results in pollution of farmland and water supplies'. Tescopoly www.tescopoly.org

Fish

'Imagine what people would say if a band of hunters strung a mile of net between two immense all-terrain vehicles and dragged it at speed across the plains of Africa. This fantastical assemblage, like something from a Mad Max movie, would scoop up everything in its way: predators, such as lions and cheetahs, lumbering endangered herbivores, such as rhinos and elephants, herds of impala and wildebeest, family groups of warthog and wild dog. Pregnant females would be swept up and carried along, with only the smallest juveniles able to wriggle through the mesh.

'Picture how the net is constructed, with huge metal roller attached to the leading edge. This rolling beam smashes and flattens obstructions, flushing creatures into the approaching filaments. The effect of flushing a huge iron bar across the savannah is to break off every outcrop, uproot every tree, bush and flowering plant, stirring columns of birds into the air. Left behind is a strangely bedraggled landscape resembling a harrowed field. The industrial hunter-gatherers now stop to examine the tangled mess of writhing dead creatures behind them. There are no markets for about a third of the animals they have caught because they don't taste too good, or because they are simply too small or too squashed. This pile of corpses is dumped on the plain to be consumed as carrion.

'This efficient but highly unselective way of killing animals is known as trawling.' The End of the Line, Charles Clover.

'Shrimp fisheries have the highest by-catch level: approximately 85% of the catch is species other than shrimp.' *Greenpeace.*

Our oceans and our fish stocks are in immense danger. Yet this issue is overlooked simply because we can't see what's happening, so don't challenge it. As we don't challenge it, there is no political will to react to the crisis. The problem is also astoundingly complicated and in the light of very little monitoring or information on what is happening, it is extremely difficult for consumers to know how to respond. To avoid harmful systems with animal farming, you don't have to be an expert on husbandry, all sorts of schemes have started like the organic food movement to supply the consumer with accredited certification systems that you can trust. Apart from the Marine Stewardship Council, barely any such schemes exist for fish. So trying to buy fish ethically is a mine field, yet the destruction and devastation of the oceans far outweighs what is happening on land and is far more urgent. In the light of the overwhelming situation, I am not going

to attempt to explain everything, I am going to try and tell you the worst to avoid and the best to follow. If you do want to find out more read the ground-breaking book by Charles Clover *The End of the Line* or the Marine Conservation Society's *Good Fish Guide* – they will supply you with the full horrific facts and what you can do.

Let's start with some, and I stress just some, of the shocking facts. In the UK our wild salmon and trout stocks have depleted by 70% in the last 30 years. The alternative industrialised fish farms that have emerged are causing untold damage by spreading disease to what remains of the wild stocks, and polluting the rivers. Organically certified fish farms are beginning to tackle some of these issues and are a massive improvement but nothing can beat managing our rivers to allow stocks to replenish, so that we can catch fish sustainably from the wild.

There are many ocean species of fish that are, right now, under severe threat from extinction. Often

> *"A little more optimistically: herring is a rare example of a success that can be achieved when politicians act on what the scientists are telling them."*

the only one known about is cod, particularly from the North Sea. Newfoundland once had one of the greatest stocks of cod in the world; its story drives home the horror of over fishing. Cod was fished to the brink of extinction and no matter how much the authorities tried to replenish the stock, it wasn't possible.

Canadians define 'collapse' of a fish stock as being a reduction to 10% of the original spawning biomass. In 2003 North Sea cod stocks were estimated at 53,000 tonnes. Charles Clover didn't manage to get an answer out of the International Council for the Exploration of the Sea (ICES) as to the original level of cod stocks in the North Sea but Ransom Myers of Dalhousie University, Canada estimated that it was once 7 million tonnes. It is therefore reasonable to conclude that stocks of cod in the North Sea have been reduced by about 90%. This should mean that there is a ban on cod fishing in the North Sea as there was in Canada in the same circumstances. The situation is so bad that since 2003 the ICES had called for a ban not only on cod fisheries but on fisheries that catch cod as their by-catch. The EU implemented a recovery plan but allowed fishing to continue, which is delaying the recovery of North Sea cod stocks.

Continuing with this extremely depressing tale: within the last 100 years there were common skate in the British waters, which, when hung by the gills, were the height of a man. Skate is now probably extinct in the North Sea. North Sea mackerel stocks collapsed in the 1970s and have never come back. In some areas plaice, sole and cod are classed as outside safe biological limits by the ICES. Plaice can reach 40 years old but will be lucky to reach 6 these days.

The last estimate for the total world fish catch was 5 years ago. Of the 78.4 million tonnes a year, some 6.8 million tonnes, is by-catch. These are the non-targeted species caught by accident, to be thrown over the side dead. The majority of these are marine mammals, sharks, turtles, birds and juvenile fish. The fishing gear or method used is responsible for this, and it could be avoided. Some by-catch could also be eaten rather than wasted.

Large-scale commercial fishing is the problem of course, but it's the small fishers and communities that are getting worst hit. The traditional small family-run businesses that only use local day boats are ruled by the weather, which allows for stocks to rest. They can't manage huge trawler nets, and instead of using sophisticated radar equipment

that ensures no fish has a chance of escaping, they rely on traditional techniques that allow for some fish to get away, which of course we need, or how else are they going to produce the next generation? As the fish stocks deplete, the big boats go further and further out to sea, penetrating deeper and deeper in the water, so there is little escape for any fish. As European fisheries collapse we spread across the globe targeting the fish that poorer nations rely on for survival, and buying their quotas (or 'pirate' ships just blatantly steal them). These peoples' traditional techniques work in harmony with maintaining stock levels, but we are imposing our disastrous industry on these countries to feed our never-ending greed for fish at any cost.

A little more optimistically: herring is a rare example of a success that can be achieved when politicians act on what the scientists are telling them. The stock collapsed in the 1970s, a ban for 4 years allowed them to replenish though not to their post-war level. Since then stocks have been slowly rising. Partly due to the ban, the fish became unfashionable, so when the ban was lifted the fish were no longer targeted. But now the Marine Conservation Society lists it as a 'fish to eat' and one Thames herring fishery is certified by the Marine Stewardship Council.

We need to allow fish to breed as we do with farm animals. We need to let fish mature and grow into spawning parents to enable the stocks to replenish. Sounds obvious doesn't it? But sturgeon is also an endangered species partly due to our desire to eat their eggs: caviar. It is downright stupid to kill any creature when it's pregnant.

Fish tend to breed at the same time of the year every year for a certain length of time. Different fish breed at different times of year, so it is straight forward to avoid breeding seasons, there is always some species of fish available at any one time. That is not to say the breeding fish cannot be bought though. It is apparently perfectly legal to catch and sell pregnant fish.

may be doing damage to the ocean or to other species through by- catch.

Sounds complicated doesn't it? But Marine Conservation Society guidelines which you can find at www.fishonline.org will provide you with all the information you need. It is pretty straight forward when you have the information. They do a handy pocket-size guide that you can carry with you at all times to ask the questions you need. For straight forward sustainable certification, look for the Marine Stewardship Council mark. This will mostly be found in supermarkets, but some restaurants are begining to take up the scheme. Of course access to a good fishmonger whom you are confident you can trust, is the solution. Put pressure on them. If enough of us keep requesting the information, then no good business person will ignore us. They do so at their peril: they are the specialists in their field and if they want to survive they need to have the knowledge.

Trawling, as described at the beginning of this section is clearly destructive. But if everyone was using fishing methods with conservation, seasonality and sustainability in mind, then quite simply the fish stocks would be maintained.

In the pub, the chefs don't order the fish when it's in its breeding season, so our fish dishes go in cycles. We already have a restricted list which includes food miles (to avoid transportation pollution and to ensure fresh not frozen fish), and eliminates many methods and all endangered species. So when the fish comes back onto the menu, it's a delight all over again. It keeps things exciting, in fact it's just like the seasonal weather: how I long for the summer and spring as winter draws to a close, and then the long winter nights seem so cosy and romantic as autumn approaches.

The Duke of Cambridge buys fish according to species. The policy is intended to discourage trade in species that are severely endangered. If in doubt, just don't by it, it certainly won't do the fish any harm. It is an easier way of choosing fish, but not as simple as it might sound because method must always be taken into account or you

This would result in a great variety of species available to choose from for our table. We would buy what was available, and sometimes that would be very little if it was too stormy at sea. This would have the beneficial effect of encouraging localised individual businesses, resulting in fairer distribution of profits. This is not to suggest that we go back to extremely dangerous and often polluting methods of fishing. We can use technology to the fish's advantage and ours.

If you live near the sea there should be no problem finding a local fishmonger who buys off the local day boats which are using sustainable methods – and they should know everything about the fishermen. This will be one of the best ways of buying fish. They may catch fish that are on the Marine Conservation Society's endangered list, but if these are not deliberately targeted, and caught as by-catch by an acceptable method, this is not too much of a problem. It's not a problem because if everyone fished this way stocks would have a chance to replenish naturally.

But fishmongers who are buying directly off small fishing boats are few and far between. In London for example, they will most likely be buying from Billingsgate market where there is very little traceability. How much cod in this country is illegally landed, i.e. from an area where stocks are in danger of extinction? Possibly 50% according to Charles Clover author of *The End of The Line*. When buying from somewhere like Billingsgate you have no idea where it has been caught, so the fishmongers will have no idea either. But every now and then you will find a fishmonger who has an interest beyond their profits, who wants to maintain the fishing industry to pass on to future generations.

When you do find a good fishmonger, use them, they are like gold dust. They will probably already have queues out of the door as they will have already been discovered. It is crucial however, as with all businesses, that we know and understand from a social responsibility point of view how to hold these retailers accountable for the produce they are selling.

Supermarkets, of course, have been guilty of being shockingly cavalier about where they source their fish. They have had the knowledge and power to have a stunningly beneficial effect on the fish industry. They have known about the devastation that is being wreaked upon the oceans and have done nothing. Nothing until the consumer has begun to ask questions. So again we have proof that you have the power, as an individual to change the world. So now some credit to these superpower supermarkets (they control 80% of the grocery market and 90% of the retail fish market): some of them have really made some extremely impressive changes. With the support – or direct encouragement – of Greenpeace, the Marine Conservation Society and the Marine Stewardship Council, they have started abiding by their guidelines and certification systems. The most basic improvement is that these days you can see labels on the fish stating where and how they were caught.

How to spot a good fishmonger
- The shop should be clean and smell of fresh fish, not stinky.
- All the fish are labelled to their area of capture.
- They must be able tell you how the fish was caught.
- They don't make you feel small for asking and will answer any questions.
- They will have a limited selection; and not try to carry all fish all the time.
- They should be able to prepare whole fish for you.
- They should be able to advise how to cook all the fish.
- The fish look fresh with clear eyes and no sign of rigor mortis.
- The skin should be shiny and not slimy – but will have a little mucus.
- The flesh should bounce back when you press it.

Introduction

"One of the problems with our present shopping culture is that we are not actually planning meals; we buy what we fancy and then end up not having the time or the desire to eat it."

Waste

'Since the 1960's the proportion of income spent on food has dropped from 25% to 10% while real incomes have gone up.' The Little Book of Food, Craig Sams.

Britons throws away a third of the food that they buy. That equates to 4.1 million tonnes of food.

One of the problems with our present shopping culture is that we are not actually planning meals; we buy what we fancy and then end up not having the time or the desire to eat it. For all but the very poor, such a small percentage of our income is being spent on food that we barely think about the waste. But by actually spending a little time thinking of meals ahead and using what's in season, you can become extremely creative. Some of my best meals come out of using what I have in the fridge or cupboard when it is nearly empty. Always having dried herbs, spices and a good stock of condiments will enable most store cupboard staples to be turned into a delicious meal. Throwing food in the bin, composting or not, must become sacreligious. Preparing a meal around leftovers may seem bonkers until you realise how much waste you save. All the meat picked off a carcass from the roast can be used for a risotto, and then you can turn the bones into soup or stock. If you have some mash left over, come up with a meal that will incorporate it such as bubble and squeak, soup or fish cakes. But not cooking too much in the first place is the golden solution.

Supermarkets' 'food grading' system plays an enormous part in food wastage in the UK. Carrots and potatoes with blemishes, peppers and cucumber that are not big enough are all rejected. When farmers have half their crop discarded in this way, they have no other market for it, so perfectly nutritious food sometimes rots away or is sold at a loss through wholesale markets. Using farming machinery that doesn't harvest the smaller stock, like carrots and potatoes, means they are left to rot in the field. All of this ensures that from fork to plate we are wasting up to half of the food we produce. But rather than thinking about how to avoid all this waste, we are still courting technologies that may create higher yields to the detriment of the environment. Waste should carry punitive penalties for business. However it looks hopeful that the realisation we live on a planet with limited resources is finally hitting home; it is our duty to protect every inch of what is left.

Packaging

'Grocery packaging still makes up roughly a quarter of household waste, and the UK's biggest supermarkets distribute some billions of plastic bags, which end up in landfill. Even degradable bags are only a very small step, as they will still predominantly go to landfill sites where the lack of sunlight and oxygen will hinder rapid breakdown.' Tescopoly, www.tescopoly.org

How much of the contents of your bin is packaging from the supermarket? Coming back from shopping today at our local shop in Herefordshire, having used my own shopping bag and buying everything in paper bags from the greengrocer, or thin plastic from the butcher and fishmonger – I dread to think what my bin would look like if I shopped in a supermarket. Looking in my fridge, if it was all packed in plastic boxes I wouldn't be able to fit it all in, I would need one of those giant American-style fridges!

Transport

'Tesco has been massively expanding into 'Extra' format hypermarkets, which are particularly geared towards car-based shopping. The proportion of Tesco's floor space taken up by hypermarkets is three times what it was 6 years ago.' Tescopoly, www.tescopoly.org

Our present food system relies heavily on transportation and the oil industry. This is a dangerous situation. Food transport accounts for

25% of UK heavy goods movements, adding to congestion and accidents as well as pollution. It accounts for a third of all the oil used in the food chain, 20.6 million tonnes. Food accounts for 19% of carbon emissions and 7% of that comes from farming. The majority of that percentage comes from transport and agrichemicals which rely on oil, and travel vast distances in production. Organic, local, seasonal, field grown food with minimal packaging can have an enormous effect on reducing GHG emissions while benefiting wild life and the economy.

In the rural areas, where food is produced, the concept of transporting that same food from another region or even another country is ludicrous. Transporting animals to slaughter hundreds of miles away is inhumane, impractical and unsustainable. This system puts enormous pressure on our roads and increases the need to build more, paid for by us in taxes. The transport of live animals around the country helped spread the epidemic of foot and mouth disease in 2001 and it is thought that imported meat was the source of the infection in the first place. With oil running out we need to rethink our food strategies and fast.

Supermarkets tend to ensure their lorries are full when they are transporting food, and they tend to be new and pretty energy efficient so pollution per item can be minimal. The trouble is that they can't possibly use these large lorries without a centralised depot. So though the cabbage on sale in a London store may have been grown in Kent, it will have to be delivered by the farmer to the depot in Birmingham and then transported back to London. That local cabbage has travelled a huge distance after all, though it will still say 'Kent' on the label. If you are buying from a farmers' market, it will have been picked the day before and come directly to the market on one straight journey. The general thinking is that it's not possible for supermarkets to truly provide us with local food, i.e. food that has travelled little distance. Sainsbury's has only one depot in the whole of the UK.

One in 10 car journeys in the UK are now made in order to buy food. Work for DEFRA suggests that car use for food shopping results in costs to society of more than £3.5 billion per year from traffic emissions, noise, accidents and congestion.

Supermarkets

'The knock on-effect in the community of a new supermarket opening is a net loss of 260 jobs.'
The Little Book of Food , *Craig Sams.*

The supermarkets sell us a life style that suits their profit margins, not our health, environment, taste, community and certainly not artisan methods that require care and passion. As they have taken control of nearly 80% of the grocery market, they have changed the face of our country. This control has enabled them to drive our delightful varieties of fruit and vegetables into virtual extinction, since supermarkets choose fruit and vegetables based on shelf life and look, not taste and vitamins.

In February 2008, the Monopolies and Mergers Commission investigated the supermarkets for a third time. In a nut shell, they concluded there were competition issues, but with each other. Small shops and local communities seem to be irrelevant to their 'monopolies'. What chance does the small business have against the supermarkets with their free car parks, huge marketing campaigns, price wars and prime locations? Declaring that Asda, Sainsbury's, Tesco and Morrison's need to 'compete' more with each other beggars belief. The independent shop keepers that are supporting the local economy just isn't figuring in this equation. They stand no chance.

The campaigns that have been fought to prevent a supermarket being built in a town have been popular and organised. The pro-supermarket lobby talks about 'convenience' but at what cost? Campaigners know that local shops, and therefore community, will be irreparably changed. But you rarely see a town without its supermarket. This may be a town planning issue because even if the council want to fight the 'supers', they don't have the power let alone the finances. These monopolising supermarkets have endless funds to pursue their latest project, to threaten litigation and to offer to fund, for example, traffic management. Without clear legislation from the government there is really nothing that can be done to stop them. Recently Tesco and Sainsbury's 'locals' have appeared on our high street, squeezing out any competition left from the small owner-run shops. The super 'locals' stay open far later than is worth their while, knowing perfectly well, if they do, the competition will never survive. Having decimated greengrocers, fishmongers and butchers they moved on to the newsagents. In a town near me a certain supermarket is rumoured to have telephoned the local fishmonger to find out the price of the daily fish they were selling so they could undercut him and put him out of business, and they succeeded.

Supermarkets sold us the delight of all year round fruit and vegetables flown from all over the world – contributing massively to climate change and devastating other countries' eco systems. Supermarkets state that they are only catering to what we demand but these multinationals know how to sell, what buttons to press, and when they have shut down most of the competition, what choice do we have? We didn't ask for all year round food and extremely cheap meat. When it was offered we blindly accepted, believing that our government would be protecting our best interests. Supermarkets have such a huge monopoly, most farmers have virtually no choice but to supply them even when sometimes it means making little profit or even a loss. If they don't continue to supply they will loose the account all together and therefore have to fold, and they do fold, often.

It's no wonder young people are staying away from the struggling farming industry – the average age of a British farmer today is 58.

Deal or no deal? Supermarket ploys

- Farmers have to pay for promotions such as buy one, get one free. They get paid for one item and effectively have to hand over the other for nothing. A farmer has to pay to be 'preferred supplier' to a supermarket without knowing how much he will get for a contract or the amount of produce needed.
- Even after a farmer has agreed a contract price

with a supermarket, if the store decides to buy more produce, he is forced to accept a lower unit price. This is known as retrospective discounting and it is the farmers who lose out.
- If a supermarket buyer over orders or if stocks fail to sell because of the weather, the farmer is often forced to accept price cuts for unsold goods or waste.
- Supermarkets are wary that new products might not sell. To cover any losses, farmers are asked to pay for the product to appear on shelves. This is known as a 'slotting allowance'.
- Supermarkets also demand fees from farmers for popular products to stay on sale. These are known as 'pay-to-stay' fees.

Source: Times on line, *Feb 08.*

Conclusion

And the cycle of carelessness with our environment and society continues. But resistance has begun. Over the last 10 years farmers' markets have popped up all over the country, presently attracting 20 million visitors a year and creating a supply chain directly with the growers. Farm shops are more and more common and can become the life blood of a farm as well as a place for us to buy the freshest food with the least food miles involved.

Finally we are beginning to embrace growing our own food again in our gardens; for the first time in 2008 in the UK we bought more vegetable seeds than flower seeds. Waiting times for allotments are lengthening, which is due more to increased demand, than to the tragic decline of their availability.

It's easy to look at the food situation in this country and be quite alarmed, but since I opened the Duke in 1998 our food industry has changed beyond recognition. Although we have a very long way to go to create a sustainable closed loop food system, we at least have an understanding of what needs to be done. With little effort and lots of pleasure we can use our food to shape our society. By following the practices advocated in this book you will be able to make your own personal contribution to improving food from 'farm to fork'.

Geetie Singh

Sara Berg (Head Chef & Co-Author)

Spring

Starters

Parsley, Potato & Nutmeg Soup

Yellow Split Pea & Ham Hock Soup

Asparagus, Radish & Shaved Hard Goat's Cheese with Croutons & Lemon Dressing

Sea Bass Ceviche with Chilli, Lemon & Purple Sprouting Broccoli

Pickled Herring - Glasmastar Sill, Aioli or Sweet Mustard

Chicken Liver Pâté with Pickled Beetroot & Onion Marmalade

Mains

Darn of Pollock with Jerusalem Artichoke, Curly Kale & Beurre Noisette

Coley & Caper Fishcakes with Leeks & Sorrel Sauce

Soy & Sesame Baked Mullet with Soba Noodle, Spring Onion & Asparagus Salad

Poached Gammon with Jersey Royals, Spinach & Mustard Sauce

Mutton & Turnip Stew

Salt Beef with Horseradish Dumplings, Rustic Parsley & Caper Sauce

Cauliflower, Baby Leek, Jerusalem Artichoke & Chervil Salad

Penne with Spicy Kidney Beans, Tomato Sauce, Black Olives, Shallots & Marjoram

Savoury Cheesecake with Red Cabbage, Dried Cranberry & Watercress Salad

Puddings

Lemon Drizzle Cake

Dark Chocolate Pots

Rhubarb, Oat & Almond Crumble with Custard

Rhubarb Fool

BRITISH SEASONAL VEGETABLES
SPRING

ASIAN GREENS
ASPARAGUS
BROCCOLI - PURPLE SPROUTING
BRUSSEL SPROUTS
CABBAGE
CARROTS
CAULIFLOWER
ANNUAL & PERENNIAL HERBS
KALE
LEEKS

LETTUCE
MUSHROOMS
POTATOES
RADISH
RHUBARB
SPINACH
SPRING GREENS
SPRING ONION
WATERCRESS

THIS IS A LIST OF PEAK SEASON VEGETABLES
WHEN PRODUCE IS LIKELY TO BE AT ITS BEST

Dominic Bailey (Assistant Manager)

Parsley, Potato & Nutmeg Soup

A rich hearty soup full of flavour and perfectly warming on a chilly spring day. In early spring you will be using stored potatoes but as the season goes on new ones will become available. I nearly always leave the skin on a potato; when you are using organic potatoes they are full of goodness and add to the flavour as well as reducing waste.

Ingredients *(serves 6)*
- 4 tbsp sunflower oil
- 10 g butter
- 3 onions, chopped
- 3 cloves garlic, chopped
- 700 g potatoes, well scrubbed
- 500 ml milk
- 200 g flat leaf parsley, course stalks removed, roughly chopped
- 1 celery stick, chopped
- 2 tsp freshly grated nutmeg
- Salt and fresh black pepper
- 600 ml vegetable stock

Method

Start by making the vegetable stock; follow recipe on page 152, do add your washed trimmings too if you are making this fresh. You can of course use bouillon instead.

Heat oil and butter in saucepan. Add the onions, celery and garlic. Sauté for about 10 minutes but not to the point where they colour. Chop the potatoes and add to the pan. Cover with the stock. Allow to simmer with a lid on the pan, for about 30 minutes or until potatoes are cooked.

Add the milk and parsley to the pan. With a stick blender, wiz the soup until smooth. Finally, add ground nutmeg, season, and taste. If too thick add more vegetable stock.

Yellow Split Pea & Ham Hock Soup

Ham and peas are beautifully potent in this soup. It can be a wonderful meal in itself. Ham hock might be quite difficult to get hold of, so do replace with bacon or gammon. If you have cooked the gammon from page 50 then leftovers from that will make a perfect base for this. Yellow split peas can be cooked from dry, but they will take much longer (about an hour) thus using more energy.

Ingredients *(serves 4)*
Preparation time: soak overnight
- 800 g yellow split peas, soaked overnight
- 500 g ham hock, can be prepared the day before
- 1 carrot, scrubbed and finely chopped
- 1 large onion, peeled and finely chopped
- 2 star anise
- 2 bay leaves
- 2 tsp dried thyme
- 2 tbsp butter
- 1 tbsp of olive oil

Method

Wash the ham hock. Place in a saucepan, cover with water, bring to the boil and simmer for 2 hours. Set aside and leave to cool, keeping the liquid. When cool, shred the meat roughly into 1 cm strips.

Strain the yellow split peas and place in the ham hock liquid. Simmer until soft, roughly 30 minutes. Heat the butter and oil in saucepan, add all the remaining ingredients and fry until soft. Add the shredded ham hock, the yellow split peas and the liquid. Simmer for 30 minutes or so, season and serve with a chunk of crusty brown bread and butter.

Asparagus, Radish & Shaved Hard Goat's Cheese with Croutons & Lemon Dressing

The asparagus season is one of those seasons like that of strawberries that everyone still understands. It's a fairly short lived one, but the sweet tender buds make a glorious start to breaking the long barren months of January to March. Organic cheese ranges are still fairly small compared to the wonderful variety of other artisan cheese we now produce in this country. It is worth hunting out a specialist cheese shop for this dish and getting something lovely and salty.

Ingredients *(serves 4)*

- 100 g bread, cut into cubes
- 5 tbsp olive oil
- 1 clove garlic, crushed in pestle & mortar
- 10 radishes, topped and tailed
- 2 lemons, zest and juice
- 20 g chervil, roughly chopped
- 400 g seasonal leaves
- 8 asparagus spears, tailed
- 200 g hard goat's cheese

Method

Preheat the oven to 200C/400F/gas 6 and put a saucepan of water on to boil, with a pinch of salt.

In the meantime make croutons: spread the cubed bread on a roasting tray, drizzle with 3 tablespoons of the olive oil and the crushed garlic, salt and pepper. Leave in oven for 10 minutes, shaking the tray every now and again to create even browning.

Slice the radishes and place in a bowl, add lemon zest and juice, olive oil, season and toss with chervil and salad leaves and plate ready to serve.

Blanch the asparagus for about 3 minutes in the pan of boiling water, or until cooked with still some bite, depending on how thick they are. Drain and put on top of the radishes, leaves etc, divide the croutons on the plate and finally, with a speed peeler, peel strips of cheese onto the top. Finish with freshly ground black pepper.

Sea Bass Ceviche with Chilli, Lemon & Purple Sprouting Broccoli

This makes a great light starter. It will go incredibly well with knäckebröd (page 136), but it's also perfect on its own. It's essential that you have really fresh sea bass from a trusted source for this dish.

Ingredients *(serves 4)*
- 2 fillets sea bass, very fresh, pin boned and skin removed
- 200 g purple sprouting broccoli, washed and tough stalks cut off
- 2 small shallots, peeled
- 1 small red, sweet chilli
- 1 lemon, to serve

Dressing
- 1 lemon, rind and juice
- 2 tbsp olive oil
- Handful of sorrel
- Salt and pepper

Method
Finely slice the sea bass, as you would with smoked salmon. Put your sharp knife at an angle that is virtually flat to the table and carefully cut slithers off the skin. Place on a tray and in the fridge.

For the dressing, whisk together the lemon juice, rind, olive oil, finely sliced sorrel and season. Bring a pan of water to the boil and blanch the broccoli for 2 minutes and drain. Slice the shallots and chilli finely, mix with the broccoli and the dressing.

Place the broccoli on a serving plate, and put the sea bass along side, and season to taste. Serve with the remaining lemon cut into quarters.

Pickled Herring – Glasmastar Sill, Aioli or Sweet Mustard

Herring is not seen often on menus in London. It is an under-used species, but its sustainable status is not as straight forward as it may seem. Follow the Marine Conservation Society guidelines for where and how the fish should be caught; but to really ensure the most sustainable standards you want to be buying from the Marine Stewardship Council certified fisheries from Hastings or Thames Blackwater. The fishing season runs from November to March.

Ingredients – Curing *(serves 10)*
Preparation: 48 hours curing

- 1 kg herring fillets
- 500 g Malden salt
- 800 ml vinegar
- 1 litre water
- 1 tbsp sugar
- 1 tbsp salt

Method

Layer the herring fillets and salt in a large baking tray or dish, ensuring that all the herring is covered in salt. Leave to sit in the fridge for 24 hours.

Combine the vinegar, water, sugar and salt in a stainless steel pan and bring to the boil. Then let it cool completely.

Wash the herring fillets and the container to remove all of the salt. Layer in container again and pour vinegar mixture over to cover the herring. Let it sit for 24 hours in the fridge then take the fillets out. Now the herrings are cured you can add any flavouring, these are our suggestions, but feel free to experiment with your favourite ingredients.

Serving Option – Clear Pickling (Swedish – Glasmastar sill)

Ingredients

- 250 ml water
- 250 ml vinegar
- 100 g sugar
- Pinch of salt
- 1 red onion, finely sliced
- 3 carrots, finely sliced
- 4 bay leaves
- 2 cloves

To serve
- 1 red onion, finely chopped
- Crème fraîche
- A few sprigs of picked dill
- Sliced buttered rye bread

Method

Bring all the ingredients to boil and let cool. Pour over the herring and let it sit for at least 12 hours to absorb all the flavours. It will keep for at least 1 week in an airtight container in the fridge.

Before serving slice the fillets length ways. Place the buttered rye bread on a plate, put a generous amount of herring on top, sprinkle the onion over, add a dollop of crème fraîche and top with the dill.

Serving Option – Aioli Herring

Ingredients

- 300 g grated cucumber, remove the seeded centre first
- 1 tsp salt
- 300 g waxy par boiled potatoes (with the skin removed)
- 4 cloves garlic, finely chopped
- 2 hard boiled egg yolks
- 200 ml mayonnaise (page 147)
- 300 ml olive oil
- Bunch of chives, chopped
- 500 g pickled herring

Method

Put cucumber and salt in colander and allow to sit for half an hour until the water begins to come out and then squeeze out remaining liquid. Grate the boiled potato and mix with the finely chopped garlic and egg yolks and put to one side.

Mix cucumber, mayonnaise, olive oil and chopped chives then combine with potatoes and season.

Place the pickled herring in a dish and layer the mayonnaise and potato mix with the herring. Make sure the mix covers the herring completely. Allow to sit for 24 hours before serving.

Serving Option – Sweet Mustard marinade

Ingredients
- 100 g Dijon mustard
- 100 g grain mustard
- 100 ml red wine vinegar
- 2 tbsp mild honey
- 100 ml oil
- Dill, chopped

Method

Put Dijon mustard, grain mustard, vinegar and honey in a bowl and whisk until thick. Slowly pour in the oil (doing this slowly is important to prevent it separating) and add the dill at the end. Pour over the herring and leave for at least 2 hours to absorb all the flavours.

Chicken Liver Pâté with Pickled Beetroot & Onion Marmalade

Chicken livers are often wasted which is a great pity as they are cheap, delicious, nutritious and no part of any animal should be wasted. Even those who tend to stay away from offal enjoy this pâté. The chicken liver pâté has been one of the staples at the Duke for our entire 10 years, ever popular. The only thing that really changes with it is the garnish for which there are endless variations; just go for something sharp along with sweetness and some crusty bread or toast.

Ingredients *(serves 8)*
Preparation: 6 hours cooling or day before
- 4 tbsp sunflower oil
- 1 kg chicken livers, cleaned
- 1 kg shallots, finely chopped
- Handful of thyme, finely chopped
- 6 cloves garlic, finely chopped
- 100 ml brandy or whisky
- 500 g butter, soft and cubed
- Salt and pepper

Method

Take a large frying pan and get it really hot on the stove, add the sunflower oil then the chicken livers in small batches, and brown, but only for about 4 minutes, you want to keep them rare. Put to one side in a bowl.

Add the shallots, thyme and garlic to the pan and sauté till soft. Add the brandy and allow to burn off for a minute or two. Add this mix to the chicken livers.

Blend with a stick blender or food processor, while slowly adding a cube of butter at a time. Blend until smooth.

Line the inside of a 20 cm long x 8 cm deep loaf tin with clingfilm. Pour in the mixture. Place in the fridge for at least 6 hours, or keep for the following day.

You can either slice the pâté or scoop like ice cream. Serve with hot toast, pickled beetroot (see page 144) and onion marmalade (page 144). Pickled cucumber (page 146) and apple chutney (page 145) will also go down a treat.

Darn of Pollock with Jerusalem Artichoke, Curly Kale & Beurre Noisette

As cod has been so severely depleted due to its popularity, alternatives needed to be found to take the pressure off the stocks. A lot of people by now will have come across pollock or coley. We have been using them in the pub since 1999.

As you will find in this recipe and in the coley one that follows, they are great fish to cook with and most people couldn't tell the difference between the cod, pollock and coley in a blind tasting, though coley looks decidedly grey when raw. This is a simple combination of early spring ingredients that work beautifully together and is a nice easy cook.

Ingredients *(serves 4)*

- 4 darns of pollock, 250 g each
- 1 kg Jerusalem artichokes, scrubbed
- 2 tbsp olive oil
- 3 cloves garlic, crushed
- 4 sprigs thyme
- 200 g curly kale, washed
- 20 g butter
- 2 cloves garlic, finely chopped
- 1 lemon, juiced
- 2 tbsp capers
- 1 tbsp parsley, roughly chopped
- 2 lemons, to serve
- Salt and pepper

Method

Preheat the oven to 200C/400F/gas 6.

Cut the Jerusalem artichokes into equal-size pieces and put in a roasting tray, drizzle with 1 tablespoon of olive oil, add the garlic, thyme and season. Cover and roast in the oven for 30-40 minutes, until soft but still keeping their shape.

Ten minutes before the artichokes are ready, heat an ovenproof frying pan with the remaining olive oil, when really hot, place the fish in the pan, skin side down and cook until brown, season, turn and place in the oven for 7 minutes or until cooked, the flesh should be white and flaky.

Bring a saucepan of water to the boil, remove any tough stalks from the curly kale, pop it in the boiling water and let cook for 3 minutes.

Meanwhile heat 15 g of butter in a frying pan till it begins to froth and become golden brown, add the garlic, lemon juice, capers and parsley. Don't let it burn, just turn a golden brown. This is a beurre noisette.

Drain the kale and put back in the saucepan with the remaining butter and season.

Put the kale on the plates, scatter with artichoke and place the fish on top. Drizzle a couple of spoonfuls of beurre noisette around the fish and serve with half a lemon.

Coley & Caper Fishcakes with Leeks & Sorrel Sauce

Sorrel's strong lemon tang works perfectly with fish and in salads too. It grows easily in British gardens or pots and is perennial so needs little work.

Ingredients *(serves 4)*

- 1 kg coley, pin boned and skin removed
- 5 bay leaves
- Half tsp black peppercorns
- 4 lemons
- 500 g potatoes
- 100 g capers
- 50 g chives, chopped
- 1 onion
- 2 cloves garlic
- 2 beaten eggs
- 500 ml whole milk
- 200 g breadcrumbs
- 30 g butter
- 500 g leeks
- 1 onion, finely chopped
- 1 clove garlic, finely chopped
- 1 teaspoon oil to fry
- 200 g sorrel, roughly chopped
- 3 tbsp crème fraîche
- Salt and pepper
- 1 lemon to serve

Method

Place the fish in a saucepan, cover with water, and put bay leaves and peppercorns on top. Slice 1 lemon and add this too. Cover, bring to the boil and simmer for 10 minutes.

While the fish is cooking wash and cut the potatoes in half. In saucepan, cover them with water, add salt, and boil for 20 minutes or until soft. Do not cook the potatoes too much as it will make the fishcakes watery, better slightly under cooked.

Drain the potatoes. Let sit for a while so all the water drains out. Mash roughly. Remove the fish from the water, (keep the water for stock, it will freeze well) flake it with a fork, add to the mash and season with salt and freshly ground pepper. Add the juice and rind of 1 lemon, capers and chives.

Heat a pan with 1 teaspoon of oil, add the onion and garlic and cook until soft. Add to the fish and mix together. Shape into cakes, making two or four per person.

Using two shallow dishes, place beaten eggs and milk with seasoning in one and in another, the breadcrumbs. Coat the fishcakes in the egg mix, and finally the breadcrumbs. Leave to chill in the fridge for 30 minutes or more.

Heat 10 g of butter in a frying pan, and cook the fishcakes for 10 minutes on each side.

Cut the leeks lengthwise through the centre, take off the first layer. Wash the leeks and cut into 2 cm pieces. Place in a saucepan with 10 g butter, salt and pepper and cook on a low heat with lid for about 10 minutes.

Place a saucepan on medium heat, add the remaining butter, onion and garlic. Let cook gently but not colour. Add the sorrel, juice of 1 lemon, crème fraîche, salt and black pepper. Simmer for two minutes.

Place the fishcakes on warmed plates, and serve with the buttered leeks on the side and sorrel sauce on top and the final lemon cut into wedges.

Soy & Sesame Baked Mullet with Soba Noodle, Spring Onion & Asparagus Salad

Red mullet is a surprisingly under-used fish considering how absolutely delicious it is. It is succulent and meaty with big bones that are easy to manage. The meatiness beautifully complements the rich Asian tang, while creating a light and zesty spring atmosphere.

Ingredients *(serves 4)*

- 100 ml soy sauce
- 100 ml water
- 1 tbsp sesame oil
- 2 tsp sesame seeds
- 30 g fresh ginger root, grated
- 4 limes (2 to serve)
- 2 cloves garlic, finely chopped
- 25 g chopped coriander, including stalks
- 4 whole red mullet, scaled and gutted
- 300 g soba noodles
- 6 spring onions
- 8 asparagus spears
- 200 g spring greens, roughly shredded
- Sunflower oil

Method

Bring the soy sauce, water, sesame oil, sesame seeds, ginger, juice of 2 limes and garlic to the boil, immediately put aside and let cool completely. Add half the coriander. Pour over the mullet (keeping a few tablespoons of the soy marinade for the noodle salad) and place in the fridge for a few hours.

Bring a large saucepan of water to the boil. Cook the soba noodles for 7-9 minutes or until soft. Drain and refresh immediately with cold water. Top, tail and cut the spring onions in half and do the same with the asparagus spears. Bring another saucepan of water to the boil, and blanch the asparagus and spring onions, together with the spring greens, for about 4 minutes. Put aside.

Take the mullet out of the marinade. Heat a frying pan, add a little sunflower oil, and place the fish in, away from you so you don't get any hot oil on you, and fry until golden brown, about 5 minutes on

each side, being careful not to burn the skin.

Place the drained noodles in a mixing bowl, add the asparagus, spring onions, spring greens and toss in the remaining soy dressing. Serve the fish with half a lime each and some coriander leaves.

Poached Gammon with Jersey Royals, Spinach & Mustard Sauce

Pigs are wonderful, intelligent and charming creatures. They are probably the brightest animal you will eat. Yet the pig industry is almost entirely built of the stuff to give you nightmares, while our humane rare breed, free range and organic pork farmers, producing succulent pork that gives the meat the reputation it deserves, struggle to survive.

If you can't buy organic pork or pork that you know comes from a really decent farm, just don't buy it. And when you are eating out, ask for confirmation that the pork is British and has been outdoor reared as the bare minimum. When reared well what an absolutely delicious meat it is though, and gammon is simply scrumptious.

Ingredients *(serves 6)*

- 1.5 kg gammon
- 1 onion
- A few peppercorns
- 4 bay leaves
- 800 g Jersey Royal potatoes or new potatoes
- Half tsp salt
- 1 onion, peeled and finely chopped
- 1 tbsp sunflower oil
- 50 ml double cream
- 3 heaped tsp grain mustard
- 3 heaped tsp English mustard
- 1 kg spinach
- 10 g butter

Method

Soak the gammon in water for 1 hour. Drain off the water. Place in a saucepan with the onion cut in half, peppercorns and bay leaves, and cover with fresh cold water. Cook for about 1 hour covered, simmering on low heat.

Twenty minutes before the gammon is cooked, scrub the potatoes and place in a saucepan with water and salt. Boil for 15-20 minutes, or until cooked. Drain and put aside.

To make the mustard sauce: Put the chopped onion in a saucepan with the sunflower oil; fry until soft. Take 100 ml of the cooking gammon stock, add to the onions then add cream and mustard, let simmer for 5 minutes.

Wash the spinach and pat dry. Fry in a pan with butter and seasoning until wilted.

Remove the gammon from the pan, keeping the stock it has cooked in. Slice the gammon, roughly 0.5 cm thick, and serve with the potatoes, wilted spinach and mustard sauce on top.

Keep the remaining gammon stock in the freezer for a ham or bacon soup.

Mutton & Turnip Stew

Oh lovely mutton. Fairly easy to find in London but surprisingly hard to find in the country, even Wales. Sheep can graze in areas most other animals would not be happy, like in the hilly regions of the UK, where they have shaped our countryside for centuries. There is no reason why they should not be outdoor reared with little feed or intervention which means they can be a great sustainable source of meat as well as being a happy animal.

Meat reared in this way is seasonal; do not expect to be buying lamb till mid to late summer as sheep will not be giving birth till the weather is milder. Lamb will be under a year, sometimes 6 months old; hogget will be over a year old heading towards its second year and mutton is usually slaughtered in its 3rd or 4th year.

Preconceptions of mutton being an 'old tough ewe' are wrong. Well hung mutton is a far richer meat, and will be superb. We use mutton here, but you can use hogget, which will take less time to cook but has a richer flavour than lamb.

Ingredients *(serves 6)*

- 4 tbsp sunflower oil
- 1.5 kg diced mutton
- 3 onions, peeled and chopped
- 6 celery sticks, diced
- 4 cloves garlic, finely chopped
- 3 carrots, peeled and diced
- 3 large turnips, peeled and quartered
- 6 juniper berries
- 6 allspice berries
- 4 bay leaves
- Handful of thyme, picked and finely chopped
- 200 ml red wine
- 400 ml meat stock
- Salt and freshly ground black pepper
- 500 g spring greens, washed and roughly chopped
- 15 g butter

Method

Heat a frying pan to really hot. Add half the oil and then the diced mutton. Don't put too much in the pan, as you want to fry the meat, not boil it. Sear on all sides and put aside.

Heat up a saucepan, add the remaining oil, place all vegetables, spices and herbs and cook until soft. Add the seared mutton, turn heat up to maximum and add the red wine. Let this reduce for about 5 minutes, pour in the stock and reduce heat to low. Place the lid on top and allow to simmer for about 1 hour until the mutton is cooked. Taste and season.

Bring a pan of salted water to the boil, add the greens and cook for 2 minutes. Drain, toss in butter and season.

Serve the mutton stew with the buttered greens.

Salt Beef with Horseradish Dumplings, Rustic Parsley & Caper Sauce

Beef is developing a reputation as an environmentally unsustainable meat, due to its farts and burps. But it need not be such an un-green beast.

If beef is outdoor reared all year round, on land where other crops cannot be grown (eg, country estates, hilly regions and some wetlands), then it is a perfectly acceptable use of land and meat to be eating. Beef that has to be fed crops that we could be eating ourselves and reared in heated buildings is where we will be wasting copious amounts of precious energy.

So treat this magnificent animal as the delicacy that it should be; as with all meat, eat only occasionally and savour every mouthful.

Ingredients *(serves 6)*
Preparation: 2 days
- *1 kg beef brisket*
- *1 onion, roughly chopped*
- *5 cloves garlic*
- *3 carrots*

Brine
- *2.5 litres water*
- *250 g demerara sugar*
- *750 g coarse salt*
- *1 tsp black peppercorns*
- *1 tsp juniper berries*
- *3 cloves*
- *4 bay leaves*
- *Springs of thyme (if you are lucky enough to find some)*

Horseradish dumplings
- *150 g day-old bread*
- *150 ml milk*
- *5 g butter*
- *2 shallots or onions, finely chopped*
- *2 cloves garlic, finely chopped*
- *100 g bacon, finely chopped*
- *1 egg, lightly beaten*
- *2 tbsp finely chopped thyme*
- *Grated nutmeg*
- *Salt and black pepper*
- *50 g grated horseradish (if you can't find fresh use from a jar)*

Parsley and caper sauce
- *100 g flat leaf parsley, roughly chopped*
- *100 g capers in vinegar*
- *50 ml red wine vinegar*
- *50 g Dijon mustard*

Method
Put all the ingredients for the brine in a large pan and bring to the boil, let it cool completely. Pour over the brisket, making sure it is completely covered, and let it stand for 48 hours.

After 48 hours, rinse the beef and put in a large saucepan with the roughly chopped onion, garlic and carrots. Let simmer for 3 hours or until soft and tender.

While the beef if simmering, prepare the dumplings. Tear up the bread and soak in the milk for about 30 minutes. Melt the butter in a frying pan and fry the shallots till golden brown. Add the garlic and bacon. Cool and add to the bread mix. Add the egg and thyme, nutmeg, salt, pepper, and horseradish, then mix with your hands. Dampen your hands, take a tablespoon of the dumpling mix and roll into an oval shape. Put them on a tray in the fridge for 30 minutes.

To make the parsley and caper sauce, combine the vinegar and mustard, then mix in the capers and parsley.

When the beef is cooked remove it from the pan and cut into chunky slices. Set aside to keep warm while the dumplings cook. Add the dumplings to the pan one by one and leave to simmer; when the dumplings reach the surface they are cooked. Immediately dish up the beef and dumplings, in the broth (stock), with a large dollop of parsley and caper sauce on top.

Cauliflower, Baby Leek, Jerusalem Artichoke & Chervil Salad

Cauliflower was once a real staple of the British diet, but has been slowly disappearing off our plates probably due to poor cooking, but it is a great vegetable that we shouldn't neglect. Using vegetables like these in a salad is absolutely delicious and has a hearty element to it that's needed before the weather begins to warm up.

Ingredients *(serves 4)*
- 1 kg Jerusalem artichokes, scrubbed
- 2 cloves garlic
- 2 tbsp olive oil
- 1 head cauliflower
- 8 baby leeks
- 400 g seasonal lettuce, rocket or watercress, washed
- 2 tbsp chopped chervil
- Salt and pepper

Dressing
- 2 tbsp maple syrup
- 2 tbsp balsamic vinegar
- 2 tbsp olive oil
- Half tbsp Dijon mustard
- 1 small garlic, finely chopped
- Salt and pepper

Method
Preheat the oven to 200C/400F/gas 6.

Cut up the Jerusalem artichokes if they are very large, you want them in roughly 5 cm pieces. Place in a roasting tray with the garlic, drizzle with the olive oil and roast for 30-40 minutes.

Make the dressing by whisking all the ingredients together and put aside.

Bring a pan of water to the boil, add a pinch of salt. Cut the cauliflower into small florets, roughly 5 cm in size. Cut the roots off the baby leeks and wash. Put the cauliflower into the boiling pan, after 2 minutes add the leeks and cook for a further 3 minutes. Drain and refresh with cold water.

When the Jerusalem artichokes are ready, place the leaves in a mixing bowl, mix in the leeks, cauliflower and chervil. Toss in the Jerusalem artichokes and the dressing. Serve immediately.

Penne with Spicy Kidney Beans, Tomato Sauce, Black Olives, Shallots & Marjoram

Spring is regarded as a season of plenty from the land. But we find the reality of working only with organic food is that vegetables are slow to appear in our kitchens. Fresh food from this season can still be sparse and weather dependant, meaning store cupboard staple meals are essential. I love this hearty dish. You can use tinned beans if you prefer, I think there is little difference from an energy and sustainability point of view. But for taste, using dried ones will absolutely swing it.

Ingredients *(serves 4)*
Preparation time: soaking overnight
- 200 g kidney beans, soaked overnight
- 2 bay leaves

Tomato sauce
- 2 large onions
- 2 sticks celery
- 8 cloves garlic
- 2 carrots
- 2 mild chillies
- 1 tbsp marjoram
- 2 tbsp olive oil
- 25 g butter
- Half tsp sugar
- 1 tbsp tomato puree
- 2 x 400 g tin whole tomatoes
- 3 shallots, sliced finely
- 1 tbsp olive oil
- 2 tbsp sherry vinegar
- 100 g black olives, pitted (Kalamata)
- 320 g penne (80 g per portion)
- Salt and pepper

Method
Drain and place the soaked kidney beans in a saucepan, cover with water and add the bay leaves. Simmer for about 40 minutes. Drain. If you change the water like this the less the beans will give you wind.

To make the tomato sauce, chop the onions, celery, garlic, carrot and chillies. Heat up a saucepan, add the oil and butter, then add the vegetables and marjoram. Cook gently until soft (about 15-20 minutes), add the sugar, tomato puree and tinned tomatoes. Allow to simmer with lid on, slowly for 1 hour. You are waiting for the oil to separate and for the sauce to thicken.

Slice the shallots finely and place in a mixing bowl, add the oil and sherry vinegar, salt and pepper and put aside.

Add the olives and the cooked kidney beans to the tomato sauce.

Bring a large saucepan of water to the boil with a pinch of salt. Add the penne, stir with a spoon and boil for 8 minutes or as per instructions. Drain.

Now combine the sauce with the penne, serve with the shallot salad on top. If you would like cheese on top, I would recommend a hard salty cheese in the style of Parmesan or pecorino.

Savoury Cheesecake with Red Cabbage, Dried Cranberry & Watercress Salad

On a warm spring day, this feels like a summery salad dish when you really need it. Increase or decrease blue cheese and herbs to your taste.

Ingredients *(serves 4)*

Base
~ *30 g salted butter, plus a little extra for greasing*
~ *20 g sunflower seeds or pumpkin seeds*
~ *80 g digestive biscuits*
~ *60 g breadcrumbs*
~ *20 g grated Parmesan*

Filling
~ *3 eggs*
~ *230 g cream cheese*
~ *110 g crème fraîche*
~ *50 ml double cream*
~ *60 g goat's cheese*
~ *60 g blue cheese*
~ *Half a leek*
~ *2 cloves garlic, finely chopped*
~ *1 tbsp chives, finely chopped*
~ *1 tbsp parsley, finely chopped*
~ *1 tbsp basil, finely chopped*
~ *Salt and pepper*

Salad
~ *One small head of red cabbage (400 g)*
~ *2 tbsp olive oil*
~ *2 tbsp sherry vinegar*
~ *100 g dried cranberries*
~ *75-100 g watercress, washed and dried*
~ *Salt and pepper*

Method

Preheat the oven to 180C/350F/gas 4.

Melt the butter in a saucepan and put aside. Place the seeds, digestive biscuits and breadcrumbs in a food processor and combine. Slowly add the melted butter and continue mixing. Add the Parmesan.

Grease a 20 cm flan tin with a little butter. Push the breadcrumb mix into the base of the tin, making sure it is completely covered and flat. Place in the oven for 10 minutes. Take out and allow to cool. Leave the oven on.

Make the filling by placing the eggs in a bowl, beat with a whisk, add cream cheese, crème fraîche and double cream. Whisk together. Crumble the goat's and blue cheese into the mix.

Clean the leek by cutting it in half lengthwise and washing it under cold water. Remove the outer layer and the very green end and root. Finely slice. Add the leek, garlic and all the herbs to the egg cream mix. Season, remembering that blue cheese is quite salty.

Fold the mix together and spoon on top of the base. Bake in the oven for 30-40 minutes. Test the cheesecake by shaking it; it should not wobble or look runny in the middle.

Allow to cool and while the cheesecake is cooling, make the cabbage salad.

Finely shred the red cabbage (removing the stalk). This can be done by hand or with a mandolin; it needs to be very thin. Put in a bowl, add the olive oil and sherry vinegar, and put aside.

Soak the cranberries in hot water. After two minutes, drain and add to the red cabbage with the watercress. Season and combine.

Lemon Drizzle Cake

In Spring lemons can be the saving grace for puddings when there is little else around except dried fruits. This cake is home-cooked comfort food, par excellence.

Ingredients *(serves 8)*
- *250 g unsalted butter, at room temperature*
- *220 g caster sugar*
- *1 tsp vanilla essence*
- *4 medium eggs*
- *Zest and juice 6 unwaxed lemons*
- *200 g self-raising flour*
- *1 tsp baking powder*
- *Half tsp salt*
- *50 g ground almonds*
- *100 g caster sugar*
- *150 g crème fraîche, to serve*

Method
Preheat the oven to 180C/350F/gas 4. Grease a 20 cm cake tin.

Cut the butter into cubes, place in a large bowl and add the sugar and vanilla essence. Beat the butter and sugar until pale and creamy. Add the eggs one at a time, whisking vigorously between each one. Add the zest and juice of 3 lemons. Don't worry if it separates: it will all come together again.

In another bowl mix the flour, baking powder, salt and ground almonds. Fold the flour into the batter using a spatula until combined. Pour the mix into the tin. Place in the oven for 50 minutes -1 hour. Check the cake is cooked by inserting a skewer or a knife which should come out clean.

While the cake is baking, make the syrup. Place the juice and zest of the 3 remaining lemons in a saucepan with the sugar. Bring to the boil and let simmer for five minutes. Put aside. When the cake is cooked place on a rack. Make holes all over the cake with a cocktail stick and pour the syrup over. When cool, cut and serve on the plate with a dollop of crème fraîche.

Dark Chocolate Pots

Rich and creamy, delectable on its own or served with cardamom biscotti for an extra treat. It is of course essential that you use Fairtrade chocolate to ensure the cocoa farmers are getting a fair deal while you enjoy your delicious pudding.

Ingredients *(serves 4)*
- *170 g 70% dark chocolate*
- *200 ml double cream*
- *110 ml milk*
- *2 egg yolks*
- *100 g icing sugar*

Method
Put the chocolate in a bowl and melt over a saucepan of simmering water. While this is melting, mix the cream, milk and egg yolks in a large bowl. Sieve the icing sugar into the cream mix.

While the chocolate is still hot, add this to the cream mix and whisk. If it does not thicken up, place back over simmering water for a few minutes while whisking.

Pour into ramekins, cups or glasses, and put them in the fridge. Serve on their own or with biscotti (page 108).

Rhubarb, Oat & Almond Crumble with Custard

Delicious rhubarb, with its all too brief season like asparagus, should be eaten in plenty when it's available. The almond in the crumble of this dish will really make it scrumptious and served with custard, what could be more perfect? It flies off the blackboard at the pub.

Ingredients *(serves 6)*

Filling
- 1 kg rhubarb, chopped into 2 cm chunks
- 1 tbsp caster sugar
- 25 g butter, to grease the dish

Topping
- 75 g butter, unsalted
- 100 g demerara sugar
- 75 g plain flour
- 75 g ground almonds
- 50 g rolled oats

Method

Preheat the oven to 200C/400F/gas 6.

Make the crumble topping. You can use almost any nuts you like really. I prefer almonds or toasted hazelnuts but walnuts are delicious too. Cut the butter into little cubes and rub them together with the remaining crumble topping ingredients, using your fingertips until they resemble breadcrumbs.

Butter a 20 cm x 17 cm ovenproof dish. Put the fruit into the dish, sprinkle with sugar and cover with the crumble topping. Bake for about 20 minutes or until the topping is golden brown. Serve with custard from page 148.

Rhubarb Fool

Rhubarb is the first fruit of the season so a welcome respite from the long fruitless months. We have made a traditional fool here using rhubarb as a sweet.

With rhubarb's wonderful sharpness it can be embraced as a savoury too; it will cut through the oiliness of mackerel or make a succulent chutney which works well with pork.

Ingredients *(serves 4)*
Preparation time: 4 hours cooling time
- 250 g rhubarb, chopped into 2.5 cm chunks
- 60 g caster sugar
- 250 ml double cream

Method

Cook the rhubarb with one tablespoon of sugar in a covered saucepan until soft heading for mushy, about 10-15 minutes. Allow to cool. Bring the cream and remaining sugar to the boil and remove from heat. Allow to cool. Fold in the rhubarb.

Place in 4 glasses and into the fridge for at least 4 hours, or overnight. (Pictured opposite)

Natascha Franklin (Sous Chef)

Summer

Starters

Crab Salad with Lemon Mayonnaise

Marinated Baked Ricotta, Mint & Grilled Courgette with Rocket & Walnut Pesto

Salt Pollock Brandade

Baba Ghanoush, Hummus, Parsley & Bean Salad

Smoked Ham Hock Salad with Spring Onions, Broad & Runner Beans with Mustard Mayonnaise

Pork Rillettes

Mains

Roast Monkfish with Caponata & Spinach

Grilled Mackerel Salad with Boiled Egg, Sugarsnaps, Capers & Olives

Spaghetti with Steamed Clams, Cuttlefish, Chilli, Garlic & Parsley

Lamb & Green Bean Casserole with Feta

Sweetcorn and Chickpea Cake with Black Olive, Radicchio Salad & Red Pepper Dressing

Courgette, Pea, Mint & Strong Cheddar Quiche

Wild Boar Chop with Crushed Pink Fir Apple Potatoes, Grilled Sweetcorn & Pepper Yoghurt Dressing

Chilli & Coriander Chicken with Couscous, Crème Fraîche & Tomato Salad

Globe Artichoke Stuffed with Peas, Mushrooms & Ewes Cheese with Garlic Roasted Marrow

Puddings

Natascha's Gooseberry & Almond Cake

Natascha's Lemon & Raspberry Tart

Meringue with Cherries & Mint

Red & Black Currant Cheesecake

BRITISH SEASONAL VEGETABLES
SUMMER

ASIAN GREENS	COURGETTES	PEPPER
ASPARAGUS	CUCUMBER	PLUMS
AUBERGINE	CURRANTS	POTATOS
BEANS:	DAMSONS	RADDISH
BROAD	FIGS	ONIONS
FRENCH	FENNEL	RASPBERRIES
RUNNER	GARLIC	SPINACH
BEETROOT	GLOBE ARTICHOKE	SPRING ONION
BLACKBERRIES	GOOSEBERRY	STREWBERRIES
BLUEBERRIES	HERBS:	SUMMER SQUASH
BROCCOLI	ANNUALS & PERENNIALS	SWEETCORN
CABBAGE	KOHLRABI	SWISS CHARD
CARROTS	LETTUCE	TOMATOS
CAULIFLOWER	MUSHROOMS	TURNIPS
CAVOLO NERO	PEAS:	WATERCRESS
CELERY	SHELL	
CHERRIES	MANGE TOUT	
	SUGAR SNAP	

THIS IS A LIST OF PEAK SEASON VEGETABLES
WHEN THE PRODUCE IS LIKELY TO BE AT ITS BEST

Fiona Ward (General Manager)

Crab Salad with Lemon Mayonnaise

If you get a live crab it is quite an experience but if you find it difficult or time-consuming, buy crab meat from your fishmonger. I like to mix a little bit of the brown meat in with the white meat, as the brown meat has lots of flavour. From a sustainability point of view you must buy pot-caught crab, brown or spider crab from the south coast are the ones you are looking for.

Ingredients *(serves 4)*

- 1 large whole crab or 200 g crab meat
- 1 kohlrabi, 150 g
- 1 fennel bulb, 150 g
- Half tbsp fresh dill
- 1 lemon, juiced
- 2 tbsp olive oil
- 200 g seasonal leaves
- 8 cherry tomatoes, halved
- Salt and pepper
- Lemon mayonnaise (page 147)
- 2 lemons, for serving

Method

A live crab will keep in the fridge for 3 to 4 days but make sure it's covered with a damp cloth. You should kill the crab before cooking it; if you don't, the crab will suffer, and the meat will tend to be tough and too much water is retained in the shell. Turn the crab on its back, with its legs upwards. Towards the back of the shell there is a small pointed flap, lift this to find a small hole. I normally use a steel (for sharpening knives), place the steel in the hole and with a sharp tap insert the steel until it's gone through, and you can feel it hit the shell on the other side. Turn the crab back on its claws and allow to drain.

Put water in a large saucepan and add salt. Place on high heat. When the water is boiling vigorously, drop the crab in and bring back to the boil. When the water is boiling again, cook for 20 minutes. Drain and allow to cool.

Meanwhile make the mayonnaise. Follow the method on page 147 but replace the tablespoon of vinegar with 1 tsp of cider vinegar and the juice and zest of 1 lemon.

Place the cooked crab on a chopping board upside down. Twist the claws and legs off and put aside. To remove the centre part lay the crab dark side down with the head pointing away from you and use your thumbs to push the centre body up and out of the shell. Throw away the small sac that is just behind the crab's mouth. Pull away the soft gills (dead man's fingers) that are attached along the edges. Cut the centre in four pieces, and with a skewer push out the meat into a bowl taking care not to include shell; this is a slow process. Using a teaspoon push out the soft brown meat inside the shell, and put into the bowl with the other meat.

Open the claws with a knock of the steel or the back of a heavy knife, and pick out the meat. Do the same with the legs and place all together in the bowl. Pick through the meat, make sure there is no shell. Keep the shell – it can be frozen and make a lovely crab bisque.

Peel the kohlrabi, and cut the root and top off the fennel. Slice them as thinly as you can; use a mandolin if you have one. Place in a bowl, with the dill, pour lemon juice and olive oil on top, and put aside.

Put the leaves and cherry tomatoes on plates, add some kohlrabi and fennel, put a large dollop of crab on the top and the lemon mayonnaise and lemon wedge on the side.

Marinated Baked Ricotta, Mint & Grilled Courgette with Rocket & Walnut Pesto

At the Duke, we buy our ricotta from Alham Wood Farm in Somerset. It's genuine buffalo milk ricotta, as they breed their own buffalo. Walnut pesto is a fantastic play on the traditional pine nut and basil pesto and also works wonderfully on spaghetti as a dish on its own. It will keep well in a jar in the fridge for up to a week if well covered by olive oil, so double the quantities for a meal later.

Ingredients – Ricotta *(serves 4)*
- 300 g ricotta, one piece or multiple smaller ones
- 3 tbsp olive oil
- Half mild chilli, finely chopped
- 2 cloves garlic, finely chopped

Method
Preheat the oven to 200C/400F/gas 6.

Put the whole ricotta on a roasting tray, drizzle with olive oil and sprinkle with the chilli and chopped garlic. Place in the oven for about 10 minutes to go light brown.

Ingredients – Grilled Courgette
- 4 courgettes
- 2 tbsp olive oil
- Juice of half a lemon
- 1 tbsp mint, roughly chopped
- Salt and pepper

Method
Slice the courgettes lengthways as thinly as you can. Put in a bowl and drizzle with olive oil, lemon juice, add the mint and season. Mix well to ensure the courgettes are well coated. Grill the courgettes till beginning to brown. (You could eat the courgettes raw if you like, I think they are lovely raw at the beginning of summer.)

Place the courgettes on a plate, crumble over the ricotta and spread the pesto over the top. Enjoy with a few leaves or as a side dish with some barbecued fish or meat.

Ingredients – Pesto
- 1 clove garlic
- 25 g walnuts in shells, shelled and finely chopped
- 250 g rocket, finely chopped
- 100 ml olive oil
- 50 g finely grated Parmesan

Method
Put the garlic in a pestle and mortar, grind to a paste, add the walnuts and rocket and grind in, slowly pour in the olive oil grinding the ingredients as you go. Mix in the Parmesan. Transfer to a dish and place in the fridge. You can put all the ingredients in a food processer adding the olive oil as it blends, but the flavours will be better ground by hand.

Salt Pollock Brandade

This is a wonderful picnic dish which is Spanish in origin. It is usually a cod-based dish but as British cod should not be eaten, pollock and coley are the fish we usually use.

Ingredients *(serves 6)*
Preparation: 24 hours salting

- 800 g pollock (or other firm white fleshed fish)
- 100 g coarse salt
- 4 bay leaves
- 8 black peppercorns
- 20 fennel seeds
- 400 g potatoes, cut into chunks
- 4 cloves garlic, finely chopped
- 2 tbsp parsley, finely chopped
- Juice of 2 lemons
- 50 ml olive oil
- Black pepper

Tomato salad

- 3 large tomatoes
- 2 tbsp olive oil
- 1 tsp red wine vinegar
- 4 basil leaves, torn
- Salt and pepper

To serve

- 6 thinly cut slices of crusty bread
- 2 cloves garlic

Method

Put the pollock in a bowl to fit in the fridge. Mix the pollock with the salt, bay leaves, peppercorns and fennel seeds, ensuring it is well coated. Cover and leave in the fridge for 24 hours.

Rinse the pollock thoroughly in cold water. Place in a saucepan, cover with water, bring to the boil and simmer for about 15-20 minutes or until flesh is flaky but still white. Drain and discard the liquid (this will be too salty for stock), set the pollock to one side.

While the fish is cooking boil the potatoes for about 20 minutes or until cooked. Drain, and while the potatoes are still hot, place the pollock and the potatoes in a bowl and crush with a wooden spoon, the idea is not to mash the potatoes too much, keeping some chunks. Add the garlic, parsley and lemon juice and slowly pour in the olive oil. Finish off with black pepper.

To make the tomato salad, slice the tomatoes, place in a dish and drizzle over the olive oil and vinegar and season to taste. Finish with the basil leaves.

Toast the bread and rub the cloves of garlic across the bread so the garlic dissolves into it. Place a spoonful of the brandade on the toast and serve with the tomato salad.

Baba Ghanoush, Hummus, Parsley & Bean Salad

Aubergine is such a lovely buttery vegetable and the smokiness of Baba Ghanoush compliments it brilliantly. This substantial meze can be served as a main course too.

Ingredients – Baba Ghanoush *(serves 6)*
- 2 aubergines
- 4 tbsp olive oil
- 2 tsp cumin seeds
- 2 tsp coriander seeds
- Juice of 2 lemons
- 2 tbsp fresh coriander, chopped
- 3 tbsp tahini
- 4 cloves garlic, chopped

Method
Preheat the oven to 180C/350F/gas 4.

Place the whole aubergines on a baking tray, prick and drizzle with 2 tablespoons of the olive oil, cover with foil and put in the oven for an hour or until completely soft.

Dry roast the cumin and coriander seeds in a frying pan on a medium heat until they pop. Grind the seeds in a pestle and mortar (or spice grinder or alternatively use ready ground).

Remove the aubergines from the oven, place in a mixing bowl and cover with a tight fitting plate or clingfilm. Allow to cool.

Carefully peel the skin off the aubergines, keeping all the liquid in the bowl. Finely chop the flesh and put back in the bowl with the remaining ingredients. Season and mix well.

Ingredients – Hummus
- 200 g dried chickpeas, soaked overnight
- 1 tsp coriander seeds
- 1 tsp cumin seeds
- Juice of 2 lemons
- 1 chilli, finely chopped
- 2 tbsp tahini
- 2 cloves garlic
- 1 tsp paprika
- 2 tbsp fresh coriander, chopped
- 3 tbsp olive oil
- Salt and pepper

Method
Drain the chickpeas and cover with fresh water, bring to boil and cook for about 30 minutes or until they are soft. Drain, reserving the water and allow to cool. Dry roast the coriander and cumin seeds as in the previous recipe.

Using a pestle and mortar, roughly grind the coriander seeds and cumin seeds.

Put all the ingredients in the food processer, with 3-4 tablespoons of the water from cooking the chickpeas, and blend until smooth. Add more of the water if needed. You are looking for a texture something like smooth peanut butter depending on how you like it, runny or stiff. Taste and season.

Ingredients – Bean Salad

- 200 g cannellini beans, soaked overnight
- 100 g cherry tomatoes
- 1 preserved lemon
- 2 tbsp parsley, roughly chopped
- 1 red onion, finely chopped
- 2 cloves garlic, finely chopped
- 1 carrot, grated
- 3 tbsp olive oil
- 2 tbsp red wine vinegar

Method

Drain the cannellini beans and cover with fresh water, boil until al dente, roughly 25 minutes, drain and place in a bowl. Cut the tomatoes in half.

Take all the flesh out of the preserved lemon so you only have the rind and no pith left. Slice thinly. Toss all the ingredients together. Add vinegar and oil and season.

Smoked Ham Hock Salad with Spring Onions, Broad & Runner Beans with Mustard Mayonnaise

The bean season has to be one of my favourites, not quite usurping salad leaves. It depends where you are in the season how you might treat your beans. If it is early, the runners won't need stringing (stripping the chewy seam off), but if the beans are bigger and tougher you will definitely need to do this. If they get really big and the shells extremely tough, you can just remove the large beans from inside.

With broad beans, early in the season they are very small and tender so you can use them whole. Later you will need to pod them, and for the very last ones of the season where they are very large with thick skins, you may want to remove the skin to get to the tender bean inside.

Ham hock is a surprisingly difficult cut to get hold of, even from the best butchers. Try ordering in advance. But there is no reason why you shouldn't use gammon or bacon instead. The same can be said for mustard leaves, if you can find them they are a treat, with a spicy mustard bite which works perfectly with a dish like this. Replace with rocket, watercress or even radicchio.

Ingredients *(serves 4)*

- 200 g boneless smoked ham hock
- 1 onion, cut in half
- 1 celery stick, roughly chopped
- 1 tsp fennel seeds
- 500 ml water
- 2 cloves garlic, crushed
- 4 spring onions, topped and tailed and cut in half
- 100 g runner beans
- 100 g broad beans
- 2 tbsp mayonnaise (page 147)
- 1 tsp grain mustard
- 100 g mustard leaves

Method

Soak the smoked ham hock in cold water for 20 minutes. Drain and place in a saucepan with the onion, celery, fennel seeds, garlic and cover with the water. Bring to the boil, and simmer for 90 minutes with the lid on. When cooked leave the meat in the liquid and set aside to cool.

Top and tail the runner beans and cut into 1 cm slices. Shell the broad beans. Blanch the beans and spring onions in a pan of salted boiling water for about 3 minutes, remove and refresh in ice water. You don't need to shell the beans again if they are small and new.

Now remove the ham hock from the liquid (you can keep the liquid for use as stock in another dish – it will freeze). Shred the meat as fine as you can and place in a mixing bowl with the beans, spring onions and season with salt and pepper. Make the mayonnaise (page 147).

Mix the mayonnaise with the grain mustard. Put the mustard leaves on a plate with the ham hock and beans on top with a generous dollop of mayonnaise.

Pork Rillettes

A pâté style dish that's easy to make. There is a long wait before it's ready to eat, but the results are well worth it.

Ingredients *(serves 4)*
Preparation: 5 hours for next day serving
- *300 g pork shoulder*
- *200 g pork belly, rindless*
- *150 g pork fat or lard*
- *250 ml water*
- *4 bay leaves*
- *4 cloves*
- *4 sprigs thyme*
- *6 peppercorns*
- *Half tsp mace*
- *2 allspice*
- *Salt*

Seasoning
- *Half tsp ground allspice*
- *1 tsp ground mace*
- *Half tsp freshly ground nutmeg*
- *Salt and freshly ground black pepper*

Method
Cut the pork shoulder and belly into 1 cm cubes.

Put the fat and water in a saucepan, add the meat and the first set of herbs and spices and bring to the boil. Allow to simmer on a very low heat, only slowly bubbling, for about 5 hours.

Remove the bay leaves, cloves and thyme. Shred the meat with 2 forks. Season with the second set of spices.

Place either in 4 ramekins or one shallow serving dish, cover with greaseproof paper and, when cooled, leave in the fridge for at least 24 hours.

Serve with toast, gherkins or pickled cucumber (page 146) and pickled onion.

Roast Monkfish with Caponata & Spinach

Monkfish has become a tremendously popular restaurant fish, though less 'on- trend' these days. Of course, as a result it is now over fished and depleted. At the Duke for our entire 10 years, we have omitted it from our menu. But to our utter delight, this year it has been given MSC rating 3 in the English and Bristol Channels and our fishers from those areas tell us stock is plentiful. So, we occasionally grace our menu with this most ugly of species.

Ingredients *(serves 4)*

- 4 small monkfish tails on the bone, approximately 200 g per tail
- 5 g butter
- Half tbsp sunflower oil
- Salt and black pepper

Caponata

- 3 medium aubergines (about 400 g per aubergine, or 1.2 kg in total)
- 1 tbsp salt
- 5 tbsp olive oil
- 2 onions, finely chopped
- 2 cloves garlic, finely chopped
- 2 sticks celery, finely chopped
- 2 small red chillies
- 2 bay leaves
- 4 large fresh ripe tomatoes
- 50 ml sherry vinegar
- 2 tbsp capers in vinegar
- 2 tbsp Kalamata black olives, stoned
- 2 sprigs basil, picked and torn
- 2 sprigs oregano or marjoram, picked and torn
- Black pepper
- 5 g butter
- 800 g spinach, washed
- Salt and pepper to taste

Method

Wash the aubergines, cut the tops off and discard. Cut into 1 cm cubes and place in a colander, sprinkle with the salt and mix. Leave for at least 10 minutes, to draw out excess water.

Put a saucepan on a medium heat, add a tablespoon of olive oil, and then the onions, garlic, celery, chillies and bay leaves. Fry for about 20 minutes.

Heat a large frying pan with a tablespoon of oil. Fry the aubergines in four batches using a tablespoon of oil each time (so that the cubes have enough space in the pan to brown). When golden brown all over, place in the saucepan with the other vegetables.

Cut the tomatoes roughly and add to the saucepan; add the sherry vinegar. Simmer for 30 minutes, stirring occasionally.

While that is cooking, prepare the monkfish; cut the flesh off the bone (keep bone for stock – it will freeze), cut off the shiny "skin" that covers the fish and discard. Put the tails on a plate, season with a little salt and black pepper.

Place a frying pan on medium heat, add sunflower oil and butter. When the butter starts frothing place the fish in the pan. Brown on all sides and cook 15 minutes or until cooked; test by inserting a knife, which should go in easily.

While the fish is cooking, add the drained capers, olives, torn basil and oregano to the caponata. Taste and season. Melt the butter in a saucepan, add the spinach and wilt for about 2 minutes. Drain the spinach again.

Place the caponata on plates. Put the spinach on top and then the monkfish. Drizzle with olive oil.

Grilled Mackerel Salad with Boiled Egg, Sugarsnaps, Capers & Olives

We have used grilled fresh mackerel for this salad but if you barbecue the fish it will add extra flavour. Choose hand line-caught mackerel, preferably MSC certified.

Ingredients *(serves 4)*
- 2 whole mackerel, gutted (approx 300 g each)
- 4 eggs
- 200 g sugarsnap peas, washed, topped and tailed
- 2 tbsp capers in vinegar, drained and rinsed
- 2 tbsp Kalamata olives, stoned
- 600 g seasonal leaves, washed
- 100 g seasonal herbs, washed and picked (e.g. parsley and sorrel)

Dressing
- 1 tbsp red wine vinegar
- 2 tbsp olive oil
- 1 tbsp grain mustard
- 1 small shallot, finely chopped

Method

Grill the mackerel for 6 minutes on each side or until cooked through. (You can do this on a barbecue if the weather holds out.) Remove the flesh and the skin from the bone, do this carefully as there as lots of small bones. Flake the flesh into generous chunks.

Place the eggs in a pan of boiling water and boil for 6 minutes. Then cool quickly in cold water; peel and put aside.

Place all the ingredients for the dressing, except the shallot, in a bowl and whisk together. Add the shallots at the end.

Bring a little more water to the boil in the pan, add the sugarsnap peas and boil for about two minutes. They should still be crunchy. Drain, cool in cold water. Mix the sugarsnaps, capers, olives, seasonal leaves and herbs in a bowl with the salad dressing.

Place the salad on plates. Sprinkle the mackerel on top, cut the eggs in quarters and distribute on the plates.

Spaghetti with Steamed Clams, Cuttlefish, Chilli, Garlic & Parsley

This has to be one of my favourite dishes of all – I could eat it every day. Cuttlefish is very messy to clean, so I would suggest you get your fishmonger to do it for you. But it can be fun to do it yourself.

Ingredients *(serves 4)*
- 1 cuttlefish, cut into 1 cm strips
- 200 g spaghetti
- 1 tsp salt
- 3 tbsp olive oil
- 80 g clams, rinse under cold water
- 1 red chilli, finely chopped
- 2 cloves garlic, finely chopped
- 100 ml dry white wine
- 2 tbsp parsley, finely chopped
- 1 lemon

Method

First prepare the cuttlefish. Wearing an apron and an old top, place the cuttlefish in a bowl with cold water, cut off the tentacles just above the head, rinse and put aside. With your bowl of cold water sitting in the sink, pull out the inner body very gently. There's a ball of ink inside so be careful, if you burst the ball you will have black ink everywhere and that's no fun and very messy. Throw away the inside.

You will be left with a tube, cut it open, and peel off the skin, rinse and then slice into 1 cm strips. Cut up the tentacles too.

Bring a large saucepan of water to the boil with a pinch of salt. When it's boiling add the spaghetti and boil for 7-9 minutes.

Meanwhile, get another saucepan very hot, add the olive oil, the clams, cuttlefish, chilli and garlic, toss for 30 seconds, then add the white wine. Cover with a lid and leave for about 5 minutes.

Drain the spaghetti and add to the clams, season and add the parsley. When all the clams are open, it is ready. Discard any clams that haven't opened.

Serve with a wedge of lemon.

Lamb & Green Bean Casserole with Feta

Sourcing seasonal field grown lamb makes this a late summer dish. But it will work just as well with hogget or mutton, just add 20 minutes extra cooking time.

Ingredients *(serves 4)*
- 1 tbsp olive oil
- 1 kg diced shoulder or neck of lamb
- 2 carrots, chopped
- 2 white onions, chopped
- 5 cloves garlic, finely chopped
- 1 bunch of thyme
- 200 ml red wine
- 240g tin tomatoes
- 1 tsp tomato puree
- 3 bay leaves
- 1 cinnamon stick
- 200 ml meat stock (page 152)
- 500 g green beans, broad, runner or French
- 200 g feta cheese
- Crusty bread or cooked waxy potatoes (like pink fir apple)

Method
Take a large saucepan and heat the oil until almost smoking.

Fry the lamb, making sure it's browned on all sides. Add the carrots, onions, garlic and thyme and fry for about 10 minutes. Add wine and let it reduce for a few minutes. Add the tinned tomatoes, puree, bay leaves and cinnamon. Stir and then add the stock. Put a lid on the saucepan and leave to simmer for about 40 minutes.

Add the beans and let cook for a further 10 minutes, taste and season.

Serve with feta cheese crumbled over the top of the stew and either crusty bread or waxy potatoes.

Sweetcorn and Chickpea Cake with Black Olive, Radicchio Salad & Red Pepper Dressing

A vegetarian 'patty' or 'cake' is a fast seller in the pub, which turns the head of many a meat eater. Not surprising though, it's a wonderful flavoursome and satisfying meal.

Ingredients *(serves 4)*
Preparation: 12-24 hours soaking of chickpeas
- 200 g chickpeas, soaked overnight
- 2 fresh corn on the cob
- 1 red onion
- 4 cloves garlic
- 2 small sweet red chilli
- 1 tbsp basil
- 1 tbsp coriander
- 4 tbsp olive oil
- Juice of 2 lemons

Dressing
- 2 red peppers
- Seasoning

Salad
- 1 head of radicchio, leaves removed and washed, 100 g
- 100 g black Kalamata olives
- 1 tbsp basil
- 1 tbsp coriander

Method
Drain and wash the chickpeas, put in a saucepan and cover with water. Bring to the boil and let simmer for 40 minutes or until soft. Drain and blend coarsely in a food processor or with a stick blender. Put aside in a bowl.

Stand the sweetcorn upright in a bowl and cut down to get the kernels off. Finely chop the red onion, garlic, chilli and sweetcorn kernels, heat a tablespoon of olive oil in a pan and fry until cooked. Add the fried vegetables to the chickpea puree and mix well. Chop the basil and coriander and add, with the lemon juice, to the mix, which should be like a wet dough. Taste and season with salt and pepper.

Preheat the oven to 200C/400F/gas 6.

Make 8 cakes out of the mixture. Put in the fridge for 30 minutes.

Meanwhile place the red peppers in a roasting tray, drizzle with a tablespoon of olive oil and a pinch of rock salt. Place in the oven for 20-30 minutes, or until their skins blacken.

Take the peppers out, put in a bowl, and cover with clingfilm for a few minutes. Keeping any liquid you create, remove all the peel and seeds and discard. With a stick blender, blend the peppers, a tablespoon of olive oil and the liquid from the peppers and season.

Heat a frying pan, add a tablespoon of oil and fry the sweetcorn cakes until golden brown on each side, finish off in the oven for 15 minutes.

Meanwhile roughly cut the radicchio, mix it with the remaining herbs, olives and the red pepper dressing.

As soon as your cakes are cooked serve them up with the salad on the side.

Courgette, Pea, Mint & Strong Cheddar Quiche

It's so worth being able to knock up a quiche, great for lunch, supper or picnics. You can use almost anything as a filling of course, and with a cheese-based one it is an excellent chance to finish off any cheese ends in the fridge – there must be hardly any cheeses that wouldn't work in a quiche. Leftovers of most sorts will work too, sausage, bacon, chicken, potatoes, spinach, olives, capers... The fillings we have used here have a light and summery feel.

When you are making pastry, it's a great idea to double the portions and freeze half of it for future use.

Ingredients *(serves 4)*

- 250 g shortcrust pastry (page 148)
- 2 small courgettes
- 5 spring onions
- 2 cloves garlic
- 100 g shelled peas
- 150 g strong cheddar, grated
- 75 g mint
- 3 eggs
- 3 egg yolks
- 125 ml double cream

Method

Preheat the oven to 180C/350F/gas 4.

Roll the pastry out on a floured surface, place in a 20-23 cm wide, shallow tin, pushing gently to the sides, leaving an over hang. Spike the bottom of the pastry a few times with a fork. Place in the oven for 40 minutes or until lightly brown.

Slice the courgettes, spring onions, and finely chop the garlic. Heat a frying pan, add the chopped vegetables and cook until soft. Blanch the peas and put to one side.

Mix together the eggs, yolks and the cream and season to taste. Increase the oven temperature to 200C/400F/gas 6.

When the pastry has cooled, place the vegetables and the cheese in the pastry case and pour over the cream mix. Bake in the oven for 30-40 minutes or until set – it shouldn't wobble when you shake it. Serve hot or cold.

Wild Boar Chop with Crushed Pink Fir Apple Potatoes, Grilled Sweetcorn & Pepper Yoghurt Dressing

We source our wild boar from the South East of England where it's a pest, which makes it a sustainable meat to eat as it needs culling. A delicious succulent meat from a beast which has foraged all its life, this recipe will work just as well with pork or lamb if you can't get hold of boar.

Ingredients *(serves 4)*
Preparation: few hours to marinate

- 4 wild boar chops, 250 g each
- 50 g thyme, removed from stalks and chopped
- 1 lemon, rind and juice
- 3 garlic cloves, crushed
- 1 small red onion, roughly chopped
- 50 g olive oil
- 2 bay leaves
- 2 red peppers
- 1 tbsp olive oil
- 200 ml yoghurt
- 1 kg pink fir apple potatoes, scrubbed
- 5 g butter
- 4 sweetcorn cobs
- 2 tbsp chopped parsley

Method

Leave the chops to marinate with the thyme, lemon, garlic, onion, olive oil and bay leaves for a few hours.

Preheat the oven to 220C/425F/gas 7 and place the red peppers on a roasting tray with a drizzle of olive oil and some sea salt.

Leave in the oven for about 20 minutes, until the skin starts to blacken and come off. Put the peppers in a bowl and cover with clingfilm. Leave the oven on. When the peppers are cool enough to handle carefully remove the skins and seeds and discard. Slice the peppers into thin strips, mix with the yoghurt and season and place in the fridge.

At the same time, boil the potatoes with a pinch of salt for about 10-15 minutes until they are nearly cooked.

Boil enough water to cover the sweetcorn, add the cobs and cook for about 15 minutes depending on their size.

Put the potatoes on the chopping board and smash them with the palm of your hand till they are about 2 cm thick and put to one side.

Season the chops. Heat a large frying pan and fry the chops on each side till browning. Pay extra attention to the skin, making sure it gets crisp. When you have browned the chops, place the potatoes in the same pan and continue cooking in the oven for about 10-15 minutes. Add the butter.

Grill the sweetcorn for a few minutes so the skin is beginning to brown and crisp.

Take the potatoes out of the pan and toss with the parsley in a mixing bowl.

Place one chop and some potatoes on a plate per person, pour the juice from the pan over them and serve with the sweetcorn and pepper yoghurt dressing.

Chilli & Coriander Chicken with Couscous, Crème Fraîche & Tomato Salad

This will work splendidly on a barbecue in the garden, but if the weather lets you down it will taste just as good cooked in the oven. Chicken, though a lean meat, can be lacking on the 'green' stakes as it tends to be fed on crops we could be eating ourselves which is an inefficient use of land and energy. Of course, the home-grown kitchen scrap-fed variety is ideal. It is essential that you use every bit of the animal, so freeze the giblets for gravy and turn the carcass into stock.

Ingredients (serves 4)
Preparation: few hours to marinate (or over-night)

- ~ 1 whole chicken, cut into 4 pieces
- ~ 2 chillies, chopped roughly
- ~ 100 g fresh coriander, chopped roughly
- ~ 50 ml olive oil
- ~ Juice of 1 lemon
- ~ 200 g couscous
- ~ 300 ml vegetable stock
- ~ Half cucumber, sliced in half lengthways
- ~ 1 red pepper
- ~ 1 red onion
- ~ 2 cloves garlic
- ~ 1 green chilli
- ~ 1 preserved lemon
- ~ 50 ml olive oil
- ~ 250 ml crème fraîche, to serve
- ~ Handful of chives, chopped finely
- ~ Salt and pepper

Tomato salad
- ~ 4 tomatoes, thinly sliced
- ~ Pinch of salt
- ~ 1 tbsp basil, roughly chopped
- ~ 1 clove garlic
- ~ 1 tbsp balsamic vinegar
- ~ 2 tbsp olive oil

Method

Marinate the chicken pieces with the chilli, fresh coriander, olive oil and lemon juice for 2 hours, or longer if there is time. Then put on skewers trying to use some of the chilli and coriander too.

Preheat the oven to 200C/400F/gas 6 or if you have the weather for it light your barbecue.

Place the couscous in a pan, bring the vegetable stock to the boil and pour over the couscous, wrap in clingfilm or cover tightly with a lid and leave for 5 minutes. With a fork, fluff up the couscous. (If it is still a bit hard cover for a couple more minutes.) Take the seeded middle out of the cucumber and discard, chop cucumber into 1 cm cubes. Do the same with the red pepper. Finely chop the red onion, garlic and chilli and just the skin of the preserved lemon. Add to the cooled couscous with the cucumber and red pepper, season and mix in the olive oil.

In a bowl, mix the crème fraîche with chives and seasoning.

Put the marinated chicken in the oven or on the barbecue and cook for roughly 15 minutes or until the flesh is white all the way through.

Place the tomatoes and basil in a bowl. Crush the garlic with the salt in a pestle and mortar, mix in the vinegar and oil, season and pour over the tomatoes.

Serve the chicken with the couscous, tomato salad and a dollop of crème fraîche.

Globe Artichoke Stuffed with Peas, Mushrooms & Ewes Cheese with Garlic Roasted Marrow

Globe artichokes remind me of the cottage mum and Geoff renovated after we left the commune. They had a decent-size patch of them and they were a summer treat. I have a cutting from one of those plants growing in my garden now. Stuffing them was something Sara introduced me too and I think it's hugely successful. Artichokes take a delightfully long time to eat, and it's a wonderful way of prolonging a lazy summer dinner.

Marrow is often dismissed as a disappointing vegetable, but I think they are undervalued. They also store brilliantly into the winter if you hang them in a string bag somewhere cool like a shed, after 2 weeks storage at room temperature.

Ingredients *(serves 4)*
- 4 globe artichokes
- 2 lemons, juiced, keep the lemons
- 2 tsp salt
- 4 Portobello mushrooms
- 1 tbsp olive oil
- 5 g butter
- 1 onion, finely chopped
- 2 cloves garlic, finely chopped
- 200 g peas, podded
- 2 tbsp torn basil
- 1 tbsp crème fraîche
- 100 g hard ewe's cheese, grated
- 500 g marrow
- 1 tbsp olive oil
- 10 g butter
- 2 cloves garlic, finely chopped
- Salt and pepper

Method
Preheat the oven to 180C/350F/gas 4.

Put about 3 litres of water in a saucepan and the juice of two lemons plus the juiced lemons and salt.

Wash the artichokes under cold water to get rid of insects and bugs. Cut off the stem to make a flat base, with scissors, cut off the sharp spikes of the leaves, and cut about 1 cm off the top (you will see the inner purple leaves clearly now). Put them promptly into the saucepan with the water and lemon. Do one artichoke at a time so that they don't go brown.

Put the pan of artichokes on medium heat with the lid on. When the water starts to simmer, cook for 20-30 minutes, depending on size.

Brush the Portobello mushrooms with a pastry brush. Never wash them, as they soak up water and will make the filling too wet and sloppy. Cut the mushrooms into 1 cm cubes and put aside. Place a saucepan on medium heat with the olive oil and butter and then the mushrooms, onion and garlic, and fry. Add the raw peas and cook for a further five minutes. Take off the heat and add crème fraîche and the grated cheese; season with pepper.

By the time this is done the artichokes should be cooked, check this by trying to pull off a leaf; if this is easy then they are ready. Drain and let cool slightly. Place an ovenproof dish in the oven. Peel the marrow and cut the seeds out and discard. Cut the marrow into 1 cm cubes. Put olive oil, butter, the marrow and garlic into the hot roasting tray. Season and put back in the oven.

When the artichokes are slightly cool, pull the little purple leaves from the centre and with a spoon pull off the "hairy" choke in the centre above the heart. All the hair needs to come out as it is an irritant.

Fill the middle of each artichoke with the mushroom stuffing and place them on a roasting tray and put in the oven with the marrow. Leave the marrow and artichokes in the oven for 15 to 20 minutes.

Take the two dishes out of the oven. Scatter the garlic roasted marrow around the serving plate, place the stuffed artichoke in the middle and drizzle with olive oil.

Now to eat! The main part of the globe artichoke is the heart (base of the artichoke) which is fleshy and tasty, but don't forget all the leaves surrounding the heart, which you can suck. It's fun and fiddly but with a lovely glass of wine and good friends it is the perfect time-consuming thing to do.

Natascha's Gooseberry & Almond Cake

These two recipes are from Natascha Franklin, the sous-chef at the Duke... 'You can change the fruit depending on what is in season, and you could swap the almonds for another nut. I like raspberries with ground hazelnuts or plums and apples in the autumn with pecans or walnuts. If you have your own jam, bottled fruit or home-made compote you could use this.'

Ingredients *(serves 4)*
- ~ *75 g unsalted butter, softened*
- ~ *150 g sugar*
- ~ *2 eggs*
- ~ *125 g plain flour*
- ~ *75 g ground almonds*
- ~ *1 tsp baking powder*
- ~ *Zest of 1 lemon*
- ~ *1 vanilla pod, seeds scraped out*
- ~ *300 g whole gooseberries, topped, tailed and washed*
- ~ *1 tbsp of good apricot jam*
- ~ *20 g crème fraîche*

Method
Prepare by lining a 22 cm tart tin with greaseproof paper. Heat the oven to 180C/350F/gas 4.

Cream together the butter and sugar. Add the eggs, beating in one at a time. Fold in the flour, ground almonds, baking powder, lemon zest and seeds of vanilla pod. Fold in half of the gooseberries, and spoon into the lined tart tin. Mix the remaining half of the gooseberries with jam and spoon over the top of the cake.

Bake for 40-50 minutes till golden and lightly springy to the touch. Serve hot with crème fraîche.

Natascha's Lemon & Raspberry Tart

'My mother, Elke, absolutely adored a lemon tart that she once ate at the Duke. She pestered and pestered me for the recipe. Whilst this is not the same tart that she ate I think she will love this. I dedicate this recipe to my crazy little mother with love.'

Ingredients *(serves 4)*

Base
- ~ *250 g digestive biscuits*
- ~ *130 g butter, melted*
- ~ *10 g sugar*
- ~ *1 tsp ground ginger*
- ~ *1 tsp ground cinnamon*
- ~ *1 lemon, zested*

Filling
- ~ *450 ml double cream*
- ~ *125 g caster sugar*
- ~ *Peel of 4 lemons*
- ~ *75 ml lemon juice*
- ~ *100 g raspberries*

Method
Crush the biscuits by placing in a plastic bag or between a couple of tea towels and roll with a rolling pin.

Then mix these together with the rest of the base ingredients. Press into a 20 cm tart tin, covering the sides and the bottom. Cool in the fridge.

Place the cream, sugar and lemon peel into a large saucepan, bring to the boil, simmer for 5 minutes. Add the lemon juice, and strain through a fine sieve.

Leave to cool for 1 hour. Spoon into the tart tin and leave for a few hours. Decorate the top with the raspberries.

Meringue with Cherries & Mint

A deliciously light, hot summer day pudding. Cherries were once grown in abundance in this country, but sadly most of the old orchards have been grubbed out. Make sure you hunt out a home-grown variety to support what remains of our orchards.

Ingredients *(serves 4)*
- 4 egg whites (make sure there is no trace of yolk)
- 100 g raw cane sugar
- 1 tsp oil, for greasing
- 300 g cherries, washed and destoned
- 2 tbsp mint, washed
- 50 ml elderflower cordial
- 25 ml water
- 200 g double cream

Method
Preheat the oven to 120C/250F/gas ½.

Place the egg whites in a clean, dry metal bowl, whisk with an electric hand whisk until they can form stiff peaks. Add the sugar one spoon at a time while still whisking. The meringue should be glossy and stiff.

Take a large baking tray, lightly brush it with some oil and line with baking paper so the paper sticks on the tray and doesn't curl into the meringue in the oven. Grease the paper on top as well, so the meringues are easier to lift up after cooking.

Put four generous spoonfuls of the meringue on the baking tray and place in the oven. Bake in the middle of the oven for about two hours or until crunchy on the outside but still gooey inside. After two hours take out and let cool on a cooling rack.

For the sauce, place all the ingredients, except the cream, in a saucepan and bring to the boil: put aside. Whip the cream until it forms peaks.

Place a dollop of cream on a serving plate (so the meringue doesn't slip), place the meringue on top, pour sauce on and finish with another dollop of cream.

Red & Black Currant Cheesecake

Baked cheesecake is such a delicious pudding (as well as being my mum's favourite), so it was a must for this book. We have used fresh currants here which have sharpness to them to complement the dish perfectly. The variations on this pudding are endless though. I can't think of a summer fruit or berry that wouldn't work and lemon or grapefruit with lots of zest is perfect in the winter. A tip from my friend Louise – vary the type of biscuit you use in the bottom, try ginger or ones with currants in.

Ingredients *(serves 6-8)*
Preparation: allow a few hours to cool
- 200 g digestive biscuits
- 80 g butter, melted
- 150 g red currants
- 150 g black currants
- 50 g caster sugar
- 260 g cream cheese
- 1 egg
- 3 tsp cornflour
- 1 tsp vanilla essence
- 2 tbsp double cream
- 100 ml double cream, whipped

Method

Preheat the oven to 150C/300F/gas 2.

Put the biscuits in a paper bag or a tea towel and roll a rolling pin over them till they are crumbs. Put the crumbs in a mixing bowl and pour in the melted butter, mix thoroughly.

Place the red currants and black currants in separate pans, with 25 g of sugar in each. Cook for about 5 minutes, until the berries have become a bit soft and the sugar is dissolved. Put to one side to cool. If you have more than roughly a tablespoon of liquid in each pan, pour off the extra liquid and keep to one side.

Grease a 22 cm cake tin with butter. Push the biscuit mix evenly down into the base. Put the cake tin on a baking tray and bake in the oven for 7-10 minutes. Set the tin and tray to one side.

Now with a wooden spoon, thoroughly mix all the remaining ingredients except the whipped cream and berries.

Set aside a tablespoon of each of the berries to serve. Slowly fold in the whipped cream and then gently fold in the berries.

Spoon the mix on top of the digestive base. Bake in the oven for 40 minutes or until cooked, it should stop wobbling when you gently shake the tray. Allow to cool and then refrigerate for a few hours before serving. Cut into portions and decorate with the remaining berries.

Geetie & Pace Homer

Autumn

Starters

Warm Salad of Wild Mushrooms & Pumpkin with Tapenade

Beef Carpaccio with Remoulade & Walnut Oil

White Bean, Sweetcorn & Chorizo Soup

Gravadlax with Pickled Cucumber

Roast Garlic Soup

Steamed Razor Clams with Cider, Cream, Tarragon & Garlic Bread

Mains

Fillet of Mackerel with Puy Lentils, Curly Kale, & Tarragon Salsa Verde

Baked Fillet of Gurnard, Herb Tabbouleh & Tomato Salsa

Duck Breast with Savoy Cabbage, Bacon & Chestnuts

Mussels in Rich Tomato Sauce, Garlic & Parmesan Breadcrumbs

Spicy Chickpea, Olive & Fennel Stew with Quinoa & Tahini Yoghurt

Braised Rabbit with Pearl Barley & Buttered Greens

Butternut Squash & Sage Ravioli with Pumpkin Seeds

Walnut & Cheddar Cake with Braised Celery

Roast Pork with Celeriac Mash & Apple Cider Sauce

Puddings

Carrot & Honey Cake

Port Stewed Damson Plums & Blackberries with Vanilla Shortbread

Cardamom Poached Pears with Biscotti

Moist Chocolate and Almond Cake

BRITISH SEASONAL VEGETABLES · AUTUMN

APPLES   CUCUMBER   PEPPERS
ASIAN GREENS   DAMSONS   PLUMS
AUBERGINES   FIGS   POTATOES
BEANS · FRENCH   FENNEL   PUMPKINS
   · RUNNER   GARLIC   ONIONS
BEETROOT   GLOBE ARTICHOKE   RADISHES
BLACKBERRIES   HERBS · ANNUAL   RASPBERRIES
BROCCOLI   · PERENNIAL   SHALLOTS
BRUSSELS SPROUTS   JERUSALEM ARTICHOKE   SPINACH
CABBAGE   KALE   SPRING ONIONS
CARROTS   KOHLRABI   SUMMER SQUASH
CAULIFLOWER   LEEKS   SWEDE
CAVOLO NERO   LETTUCE   SWEETCORN
CELERIAC   MARROW   SWISS CHARD
CELERY   MUSHROOMS   TOMAT...
COURGETTE   PARSNIPS   TURN...
     PEARS   WATE...
          WINTE...

THIS IS A LIST OF SEASONAL VEGET...
WHEN THE PRODUCE IS LIKELY T...

Gareth Hemsley (Shift runner)

Warm Salad of Wild Mushrooms & Pumpkin with Tapenade

If you are lucky enough to be able to forage for mushrooms use whatever edibles you find. Take great care though, it is not worth the risk of eating something you are not absolutely certain about. You can of course use cultivated mushrooms for this dish. It works best with pumpkin, though butternut squash will be excellent too.

Tapenade is a superbly rich olive dressing, it works wonders with fish, on toast, and with salads. It will last for at least two weeks in the fridge. Make sure the olive oil covers the surface.

Anchovies are becoming quite a threatened species so you do have to be extremely careful where you are buying from these days. The only place I think it's wise to get them at the moment is from the supplier Fish 4 Ever. They can be found in most good shops or stores. If you can't get hold of sustainable ones, make the tapenade without them, it will still be delicious, just add extra salt.

Ingredients *(serves 4)*
- 500 g mixed wild mushrooms such as field mushroom, giant puff ball or parasol, in thick slices
- 1 small pumpkin, approx 1 kg
- 2 tbsp olive oil
- 50 g butter
- 1 red onion, finely chopped
- 1 clove garlic, finely chopped
- 1 tbsp parsley, roughly chopped
- Salt and pepper
- 300-400 g watercress

Tapenade
- 1 clove garlic
- 100 g black Kalamata olives, pitted
- 20 g anchovy, in oil (only if you can find sustainable ones)
- 2 red chillies, to taste
- 100 ml good quality olive oil
- 2 tbsp flat parsley, washed and roughly chopped

Method
Preheat the oven to 180C/350F/gas 4.

Clean the mushrooms by picking through them and brushing them with a pastry brush if needed – don't wash them because they will soak up all the water.

Wash the pumpkin, cut it in half, and take the seeds out with a spoon. Cut into wedges and place in a roasting tray, drizzle with the olive oil, salt and freshly ground black pepper. Roast for 30 minutes, depending on the size of your pumpkin.

Heat a frying pan, add the butter, onion and garlic, and fry for 2 minutes. On a medium heat, add the cleaned mushrooms and fry for about 3-5 minutes, season and add the parsley.

For the tapenade, crush and chop the garlic. Chop the olives, anchovy and chillies. You can make this either coarse or as fine as you like. I prefer it somewhere in the middle. Add olive oil, put in a bowl and mix in finely chopped parsley.

Wash the watercress, cut off the tough ends of the stalks and dry.

Serve the pumpkin slices whole, with the mushrooms scattered over the top. Toss the watercress in the tapenade and serve on the side.

Beef Carpaccio with Remoulade & Walnut Oil

Your beef must come from a trusted producer who will hang it well and rear it with love and concern for the animal and the environment. There is no need to cut beef out altogether for environmental or welfare reasons, just eat occasionally, as with all meat, and only buy the very best (Soil Association certified of course).

I fell in love with remoulade when I was living in Amsterdam and didn't find anyone who could make it well till I met Sara. She has a knack with these simple classic dishes – she's a dab hand at coleslaw too.

Walnut oil – this is a hard one, I wouldn't use it unless you can find a really good source. My father, in France, has his own walnuts pressed by his neighbour Madame Francoise Astor, and it is absolute heaven! He only has a few fruiting trees at the moment, but has planted a walnut grove, so there will be an abundance in the future. I can't wait. When you have tasted freshly pressed virgin walnut oil you realise most of what you have been eating is rancid. Walnut oil should come in a dark container and live in a cold place or in the fridge.

Ingredients *(serves 4)*
- 400 g beef fillet
- 1 tbsp Dijon mustard
- Sunflower oil
- Salt and freshly ground pepper
- 1 tbsp fresh walnut (or olive) oil

Mayonnaise
- 1 egg yolk
- Half tsp Dijon mustard
- 1 tsp red wine vinegar
- Pinch of salt
- Approx 100 ml olive oil

Remoulade
- 1 small celeriac
- 1 heaped tsp grain mustard
- 2 tbsp mayonnaise
- 1 clove garlic, finely chopped
- 2 tsp parsley, finely chopped
- Salt and pepper

Method
Take a large pan and heat it till it's truly hot, until it starts to smoke; while that's heating season the fillet with salt and pepper. Put a little sunflower oil in the pan and slowly place the beef facing away from you into the pan. Sear all sides (very important to keep all the lovely juices in) until golden brown. Remove, place on a tray and rub all over with the mustard.

Let it cool and then wrap in clingfilm and put in the fridge for 30 minutes.

To make the mayonnaise put all the ingredients except the oil in a small bowl and blend with a hand blender. Slowly add the oil till you have reached a thick texture.

To make the remoulade, peel the celeriac and slice into as thin strips as possible. (You can grate it but this makes this dish a bit more watery.) Place all the ingredients in a bowl and mix well with the mayonnaise.

Slice the beef as thinly as you possibly can, it is worth taking time over this, and serve with remoulade on the side. Drizzle walnut oil over the whole dish.

White Bean, Sweetcorn & Chorizo Soup

This is such a delicious soup, but you can serve it as a stew as well – use less liquid, don't mash the beans and cut the chorizo chunkier. You can also add fresh green beans or dried broad beans. We recommend Brindisa's cooking chorizo if you can get it.

Ingredients *(serves 4)*

- 200 g white beans (cannellini, haricot or butter beans), soaked overnight
- 4 bay leaves
- 2 tsp olive oil
- 2 onions, finely chopped
- 1 small celeriac, finely chopped
- 2 carrots, finely chopped
- 2 sticks celery, finely chopped
- 4 cloves garlic, finely chopped
- 2 sprigs rosemary, finely chopped
- 4 sprigs thyme, leaves removed from stalks
- 100 g cooking chorizo
- 2 medium whole sweetcorn, kernels removed
- 1.5 litre vegetable stock (page 152 or use a cube)

Method

Drain the white beans, place in a saucepan with the bay leaves, cover with cold water. Bring to the boil and let simmer for 40 minutes to 1 hour or until the beans are soft. When they are cooked, drain and mash roughly, still leaving some of the beans whole.

With a little oil in a large bottomed saucepan, sauté the onions, celeriac, carrots, celery, garlic, and the herbs until light brown and soft.

Quarter the chorizo length ways, then chop into 1 cm slices. Fry with the vegetables until the chorizo browns. Add the sweetcorn to the vegetables. Add the cooked white beans and vegetable stock and leave to simmer for 20 minutes. Season. Serve with crusty bread.

Gravadlax with Pickled Cucumber

This is such a simple dish to make and you can adjust the flavours to your taste. The fish will freeze really well after it's been marinated so increase the quantities if you like.

Wild salmon stocks are so dangerously low; we shouldn't be eating it at all. Fish farming is not the ideal solution, being partly accountable for the cause of decline in wild stock. The only sustainable way to eat salmon is if it is organically farmed to Soil Association standards. We use Soil Association organic farmed salmon at the pub when we can't get hold of other fish due to our extremely restrictive fish policy. I think it is a fish that should be eaten only occasionally, as from an environmental point of view, even organically farmed is not ideal.

Ingredients *(serves 6 big portions)*
Preparation time – 2 days curing
- *500 g organically farmed side of salmon*
- *3 tbsp coarse salt*
- *4 tbsp caster sugar*
- *1 bunch fresh dill, chopped*
- *1 tsp fennel seeds*
- *1 tsp white peppercorns*

Method

Remove any bones from the salmon fillet. Cut it evenly in half lengthwise so each piece can sit one on top of the other like a sandwich with the skin up.

Place all ingredients in a pestle and mortar and grind gently together to bring out the flavours.

Place one fillet, skin side down, on a plate and spread all the mixture on top of it. Place the other fillet, skin side up over the first piece covering it as evenly as you can. Wrap in clingfilm or tightly in wax paper and leave in the fridge for 2 days, turning after 24 hours so that the other side gets marinated.

Wash the salmon thoroughly. With your knife virtually horizontal, very slightly at slant, slice as thinly as you can creating long thin slithers. Take your time at this stage. You are looking for slices similar to those of shop-bought smoked salmon but it's pretty hard to go too thin. Serve with pickled cucumber (page 146) and fresh dill on top with buttered brown bread.

Roast Garlic Soup

Garlic is so easy to grow at home that you can end up with far too much. This recipe will help to use up your glut. Grow garlic by putting cloves about an inch below the surface of the soil. You can grow it in a pot, from January onwards to have an all year round supply. Baking the garlic makes this a deliciously sweet and smoky dish.

Ingredients *(serves 4)*
- *4 heads of garlic*
- *2 onions, white*
- *3 sticks celery*
- *Half bunch (100 g) thyme, chopped*
- *100 g unsalted butter*
- *500 ml vegetable stock (page 152)*
- *1 large potato, roughly chopped*
- *200 ml double cream*

Method

Preheat the oven to 150C/300F/gas 2.

Put the heads of garlic on a roasting tray and cover with foil. Bake for 1 hour or until the garlic is really soft.

Chop the onions, celery and thyme. Put a medium size saucepan on the stove, add the butter and when it becomes golden brown and starts to foam, add the vegetables. Leave to sweat down slowly to bring out the sweetness.

Take the garlic from the oven and squeeze each clove into a bowl making sure you get all the flesh out. Add the garlic to the saucepan and then the vegetable stock and potato. Leave to simmer for 20-30 minutes.

Blend with a hand blender. Add the cream and serve with freshly baked bread and a drizzle of good olive oil.

Steamed Razor Clams with Cider, Cream, Tarragon & Garlic Bread

Razor clams are rarely seen on menus, in shops or fishmongers. But they are so yummy, you actually get a big chunk of flesh from each one rather than the fiddly pickings from their smaller cousins. They must be hand gathered – dredging is extremely destructive. They are an under-used species, so an excellent alternative to the usual clam. Do ensure that they are from the UK as lots are imported into this country. Treat them like other molluscs: if they don't open they are dead and dangerous to eat. Be warned, they are a sight to cook, they wiggle out of their shells.

One should also support our once-thriving cider industry and buy one of the fantastic ciders that are still out there like the ones we sell in the pub, Luscombe, Westons or Dunkertons.

Ingredients *(serves 4)*

- *12 razor clams (3 per portion)*
- *2 tbsp sea salt*
- *4 shallots*
- *4 cloves garlic*
- *4 tbsp chopped tarragon*
- *4 tbsp olive oil*
- *200 ml good local cider*
- *100 ml double cream*
- *50 g butter*
- *1 slice per person of home-made bread or other good hearty bread*
- *3 cloves garlic, whole*

Method

The clams should be closed when you buy them, this means they are fresh. And they should also have been purged, which is removing the grit from them. But it's always worth giving them another clean as grit can really spoil your dish. This is done by putting the clams in a tray of cold water (you can apparently add oat meal which will make the process more efficient). Leave them for half an hour or so, drain and rinse again. Put them in the fridge with a damp cloth over until cooking time.

Finely chop the shallots and garlic. Take a large saucepan and put on the heat until very, very hot. Add half the olive oil, shallots, garlic and tarragon. Pop the bread in the toaster. Quickly place the razor clams in the pan, give it a shake, add the cider and put the lid on. Leave about 3 minutes or until all the clams have opened (really, don't over cook the clams or they will be tough and rubbery). Add the cream, the butter and seasoning when the clams are ready. Rub the toast with the extra whole cloves of garlic and drizzle with the remaining olive oil.

Serve in large bowls with plenty of the creamy sauce and the toasted bread.

Fillet of Mackerel with Puy Lentils, Curly Kale & Tarragon Salsa Verde

Mackerel is one of the most healthy fish and becoming more and more popular. Rich in omega oil, it has a lovely full flavour. Cold, smoked or hot it is equally delicious.

Salsa verde is such a versatile condiment. It works beautifully with fish and lentils. It can be used however for bruschetta, on pasta or potatoes or just on the side with an omelette. Use any green herb you like, but the softer ones will work best. It's a great way to use up left-over herbs and as long as it's covered in olive oil it will keep well for at least a week in the fridge.

Ingredients *(serves 4)*

- 4 fillets mackerel (150 g per fillet)
- 2 tsp olive oil, for frying fish
- 15 g butter
- 1 onion, peeled and finely chopped
- 2 carrots, peeled and finely chopped
- 2 sticks celery, finely chopped
- 200 g Puy lentils
- 350 ml fish stock (page 153)
- 1 clove garlic, sliced
- 200 g curly kale (the thick stalks can be removed)
- 1 lemon

Salsa verde

- 50 g anchovies, chopped (only if you can find sustainable ones)
- 2 tbsp tarragon, washed and roughly chopped
- 2 tbsp flat parsley, washed and roughly chopped
- 2 tbsp capers in vinegar
- 1 tbsp red wine vinegar
- Half red onion, finely chopped
- 1 clove garlic, finely chopped
- 1 tsp Dijon mustard
- 3 tbsp olive oil
- Salt and freshly ground pepper

Method

Melt 5 g of the butter in a saucepan, add the onion, carrots and celery. Cook gently, covered, for a few minutes, add the lentils and fry for a further few minutes. Add the fish stock and simmer for about 15-20 minutes until soft.

For the salsa verde, place all the ingredients except the olive oil in a bowl, mix together with a spoon and slowly add the olive oil.

Meanwhile heat up a frying pan, add the oil and 5 g of butter and when they are frothing and golden brown, place the mackerel fillets skin side down in the pan. Season. Turn over after about 4 minutes and fry for another 4 minutes on the other side.

While the fish is cooking, heat up a saucepan, add the remaining butter, sliced garlic and the curly kale with a dash of water, and season. Cook for 4 minutes.

Serve the lentils and curly kale with the mackerel on top and a large wedge of lemon, accompanied by tarragon salsa verde.

Baked Fillet of Gurnard, Herb Tabbouleh & Tomato Salsa

Gurnard has to be one of my favourite fish. It has been a wasted by-catch discard for years and what a crime for such a succulent, fleshy white fish. It's an ugly thing, but for me, that only adds to its appeal. Use as you would any white fish.

The preserved lemon (page 147) in this dish is so worth having in your store cupboard. It is so versatile; I add it endlessly to salads and stews. But it has to be made a few weeks ahead.

Ingredients *(serves 4)*

- ~ *4 gurnard fillets, 180-200 g per fillet*
- ~ *200 g cracked wheat or bulgar wheat*
- ~ *400 ml boiling water*
- ~ *1 whole preserved lemon (page 147) or zest and juice of 2 fresh lemons*
- ~ *1 tbsp flat parsley, washed and finely chopped*
- ~ *1 tbsp mint, washed and finely chopped*
- ~ *1 tbsp tarragon, washed and finely chopped*
- ~ *1 tbsp chives, finely chopped*
- ~ *3 cloves garlic, finely chopped*
- ~ *Half red onion, finely chopped*
- ~ *Juice of a lemon*
- ~ *5 tbsp olive oil*
- ~ *2 cloves garlic*
- ~ *3 tbsp red wine vinegar*
- ~ *3 tbsp olive oil*
- ~ *1 red pepper, finely chopped*
- ~ *2 tomatoes, finely chopped*
- ~ *2 tbsp parsley, chopped*
- ~ *1 tbsp sunflower oil*
- ~ *Chives, for serving*
- ~ *1 lemon, for serving*

Method

Put the cracked wheat in a saucepan, pour the boiling water over it, cover with a tight fitting lid and allow to sit for 5 minutes or until all the water has been absorbed. Remove the lid and stir with a fork to make it fluffy. Leave to cool.

Cut the centre out of the preserved lemon and discard, you are only using the rind. Chop finely and add to the wheat with the parsley, mint, tarragon and chives, 3 garlic cloves, red onion, lemon juice and finally the 5 tablespoons of olive oil. Taste and add salt and pepper. Put aside.

Crush the 2 cloves of garlic in a pestle and mortar with salt, add the vinegar and slowly mix in the remaining olive oil. Put the red pepper, tomatoes and parsley into a mixing bowl and cover with the dressing finishing off with lots of fresh black pepper.

Put a little sunflower oil into a really hot frying pan, place the fillets of gurnard in the pan, skin side down, then turn the heat down to medium and let the skin turn golden brown. Turn over and fry for a further 2 minutes.

Put the herb tabbouleh on a serving plate. Place the fish on top, and finally the tomato salsa. Drizzle with olive oil, some chopped chives and serve with a big wedge of lemon.

Duck Breast with Savoy Cabbage, Bacon & Chestnuts

Go to a butcher for your duck to be sure it is as wild as possible. As with most game birds, there is wild, and semi-wild. But you don't want it intensively reared. The semi-wild ducks will have had some grain feed. When it comes to semi-wild pheasants though, they will be escapees from the ones that are intensively reared for shooting. Mallard is what you are most likely to be buying.

Ingredients *(serves 4)*
- *4 duck breasts or 1 whole duck or 2 duck breasts and 2 duck legs*
- *1 savoy cabbage*
- *200 g smoked bacon*
- *35 g butter*
- *1 onion, finely chopped*
- *2 carrots, finely chopped*
- *3 cloves garlic, finely chopped*
- *3 bay leaves*
- *100 ml white wine*
- *6 tbsp meat stock*
- *1 kg potatoes, scrubbed and cut into 1 cm cubes*
- *200 ml red wine*
- *100 g whole chestnuts (can be tinned or from a jar)*
- *1 tsp salt*

Method

Score the skin of the duck breasts in three strokes, from side to side. Don't go all the way through, only the skin. Put aside. Slice the savoy cabbage thinly and put this aside too.

Preheat the oven to 220C/425F/gas 7.

Cut the bacon into 1 cm strips. Heat up a wide-bottomed saucepan. Add the butter, and cook the bacon until crisp. Then add the onion, carrots and garlic, and cook for about 10 minutes on a medium heat. Add the savoy cabbage, bay leaves and the wine and raise the heat. Allow the wine to reduce for about 5 minutes, then add the 3 tablespoons of stock and cook with the lid on, on a low heat for about 30 minutes.

After the cabbage has cooked for 15 minutes, heat an ovenproof frying pan until really hot, add the duck breasts, skin side down (no oil or butter is needed because there is plenty of fat on the duck skin). Let the skin get golden and a bit crispy, then turn the pieces over and brown on the other side. Turn over again on to the skin side and place in the oven for about 10 minutes.

Put the potatoes in a saucepan, cover with cold salted water and boil for 10 minutes.

Take the duck out of the oven and allow to rest on a warm plate in a warm place for 5 minutes. To make the red wine gravy, put the duck frying pan back on the stove top, add the red wine, let it reduce for 5 minutes, add the remaining meat stock and bring to the boil.

Drain the potatoes.

Add salt and freshly ground black pepper to the savoy cabbage. Crush the chestnuts (just with your fingers) and stir into the cabbage.

Slice the duck breasts (add any juices from the duck into the gravy) and place them on top of the savoy cabbage, with potatoes on the side. Serve with red wine gravy.

The duck fat will keep for months in the fridge. It's great for roasting potatoes.

Mussels in Rich Tomato Sauce, Garlic & Parmesan Breadcrumbs

This recipe is easy and superbly tasty and mussels are abundant and good for you. They are farmed by being grown on ropes and rope-grown mussels are a sustainable mariculture method. When buying wild ones, make sure they are hand gathered as dredging is extremely destructive.

You can use any hard cheese that is like Parmesan, don't get stuck on what we suggest. We have put fresh parsley in the recipe, but it's not essential. It is only a suggestion if you are lucky enough to have some left from your garden or pot, or if there is still some around in the famers' markets, if not dried will do.

Ingredients *(serves 4)*
- ~ 150 g stale bread
- ~ 2 tbsp olive oil
- ~ 5 cloves garlic, crushed
- ~ 100 g Parmesan cheese, finely grated
- ~ 400 g mussels, fresh, closed
- ~ 150 ml white wine
- ~ 25 g parsley, roughly chopped
- ~ Sea salt

Tomato sauce
- ~ 2 tbsp olive oil
- ~ 10 g butter
- ~ 2 large onions, finely chopped
- ~ 2 sticks celery, finely chopped
- ~ 8 cloves garlic, finely chopped
- ~ 1 mild chilli, finely chopped (optional)
- ~ 1 tbsp thyme
- ~ Half tsp sugar
- ~ 1 tbsp tomato puree
- ~ 2 x 400 g tins whole tomatoes

Method

For the tomato sauce, heat the oil and butter in a saucepan, then add the vegetables, chilli and thyme. Cook gently until soft (about 15-20 minutes), add the sugar then tomato puree and tinned tomatoes. Crush the tomatoes with a wooden spoon. Allow to simmer with a lid on for 1 hour – you are waiting for the oil to come to the surface and the sauce to thicken.

Preheat the oven to 180C/350F/gas 4.

To make the breadcrumbs tear the bread up and place on a roasting tray with the olive oil, crushed garlic cloves, and a sprinkle of sea salt. Put in the oven for about 12 minutes, shaking the tray now and again until they are browned. Take out of the oven, leave to cool, and put in a food processor with the finely grated Parmesan, to make rough breadcrumbs.

Make sure the mussels are closed and not broken, discard any that are, clean them and pull off the beards. Rinse under cold water.

Heat a saucepan till it's really hot, add the cleaned mussels and the white wine. Cover and leave for a few minutes or until all the mussels have opened. If a few won't open, take them out and throw them away (they should be at least 2 cm open). Put the hot tomato sauce in with the mussels and serve in a bowl with breadcrumbs and parsley on top.

Spicy Chickpea, Olive & Fennel Stew with Quinoa & Tahini Yoghurt

This is a really healthy dish that's bursting with flavour. You can use tinned chickpeas but the best taste and health benefits will come from dried ones, soaked overnight.

Ingredients *(serves 4)*
Preparation: 24 hours – soaking time

- 300 g chickpeas, soaked overnight
- 2 tbsp olive oil
- 2 red onions, finely chopped
- 2 carrots, finely chopped
- 5 cloves garlic, finely chopped
- 3 mild chillies or to taste, finely chopped
- 1 tbsp chopped rosemary
- 2 x 240 g tins tomatoes
- 1 head fennel, topped and tailed
- 100 g olives, green or black, pitted
- 200 g quinoa
- 3 tbsp parsley, chopped
- Juice of half a lemon
- 200 ml yoghurt (page 149)
- 1 tsp tahini
- 1 tbsp parsley
- 25 g black cumin seeds, or toast some cumin seeds

Method

Drain and wash the chickpeas, place in a saucepan and cover with fresh water. Boil for 30 minutes or until cooked, and drain.

Heat up a saucepan, add the olive oil and the onions, carrots, garlic, chilli and rosemary. Cook until soft, about 10 minutes. Add the cooked chickpeas and tins of tomatoes and bring to the boil. Cut the fennel into 8 wedges. Add fennel and olives to the stew and season. Cover with a lid and simmer for 30-40 minutes.

Bring 300 ml of water to the boil, add the quinoa, and simmer for 10 minutes. Fluff up with a fork. When cool add the parsley and lemon juice.

In the meantime mix the yoghurt with tahini, parsley and black cumin seeds. Make sure you mix the tahini in thoroughly.

Serve immediately, in large bowls with a spoon of quinoa beside the stew, with a dollop of yoghurt on top.

Braised Rabbit with Pearl Barley & Buttered Greens

Wild rabbit is a pest and is culled. But shockingly, often it is culled and either left to the foxes or buried. This is a terrible waste especially considering we have to reduce our meat production and consumption. So with this in mind it really is a super sustainable meat to be eating. Do ensure it is wild though, if you are eating farmed it is completely defeating the object. Barley is an ancient crop in the UK, used for beer making of course, underused in cooking these days, absolutely delicious.

Ingredients *(serves 4)*

- 2 rabbits, cut into saddle, back legs and front legs (see butchery on page 150)
- 10 g butter
- 200 ml beer
- 1 tbsp olive oil
- 3 small onions, finely chopped
- 3 carrots, finely chopped
- 4 cloves garlic, finely chopped
- 1 small swede, chopped into 1 cm cubes
- 300 g pearl barley
- 800 ml-1 litre meat stock
- 3 bay leaves
- 3 sprigs thyme
- 3 sprigs rosemary
- Salt and pepper
- 400 g curly kale, cavolo nero or savoy cabbage
- 5 g butter

Method

Put the butter into a hot frying pan. Sear all sides of the rabbit, remove from the pan and put aside. Off the heat, deglaze the pan by pouring the beer into it and using the liquid to get all the sticky brown off the bottom.

Heat a saucepan and add oil, then onions, carrots and garlic, fry until soft. Add the swede as well. Place the rabbit and the pearl barley on the top and add the liquid from the frying pan, plus the meat stock. Add bay leaves, thyme and rosemary. Cover with a lid, bring to the boil, reduce heat and allow to simmer. Cook for about 1-2 hours or until tender.

Wash the greens, cut off any tough stalks, heat up a saucepan to medium heat, put the butter in the pan and cook the greens for 3-5 minutes or until al dente.

Ladle the rabbit onto plates, and serve with buttered greens on the side.

Butternut Squash & Sage Ravioli with Pumpkin Seeds

There are some dishes where making your own pasta is really worth it, this is one of them. It's not as hard as one might think, it's a dough with lots of rolling rather than kneading. The butternut squash and the buttery sage are a wonderful combination. Pasta dough freezes well, so you could double your quantities to make a different filling another time.

Ingredients *(serves 4)*

- 1.5 kg butternut squash
- 2 tbsp olive oil
- 2 cloves garlic, crushed
- 1 tsp salt and ground black pepper
- 2 tbsp chopped sage leaves
- 60 g (3 tbsp) Parmesan, grated
- 200 g rocket
- 2 tbsp olive oil
- 2 tbsp walnut oil
- 1 tbsp red wine vinegar
- 20 g butter
- 1 lemon, juiced
- 2 tbsp sage leaves
- 50 g pumpkin seeds
- Salt and pepper

Pasta dough *(makes about 1 kg)*

- 600 g 00 flour
- 1 tsp salt
- 6 eggs
- 1 tbsp olive oil

Method

To make the pasta dough' place the flour mixed with salt on a clean surface. Make a well in the centre. Crack the eggs into a bowl, lightly whisk with a fork, and add olive oil. Put half the egg mix in the centre of the flour well. Using your hands fold from the outer side of the flour into the egg. Add more egg mix as you go along. Now, knead by pushing the palm of your hands into the dough and folding together. Do this repeatedly for about 10 minutes; it develops the gluten in the dough.

Cut the dough in half and flatten it with your hand. Wrap the 2 halves separately in clingfilm and leave to rest in the fridge for half an hour. Meanwhile, make the filling. Preheat the oven to 200C/400F/gas 6.

Wash and cut the butternut squash in half. Discard the seeds, cut into wedges about 2 cm thick; leave the skin on. Place on a roasting tray and drizzle with a tablespoon of olive oil and add crushed garlic. Season, and put in the oven for about 30 minutes or until soft. Take out, allow to cool slightly, scoop the flesh off the skin into a bowl with a spoon, add the chopped sage and grated Parmesan and smash with a fork: leave it chunky. Add a further tablespoon of olive oil and season to taste.

Take the dough out of the fridge. A pasta machine is quickest for the next stage, but if you do not have one just use a rolling pin and roll the dough by hand. Place one piece of dough on a floured surface and dust. Flatten out with your hand. Put the pasta machine on thickest setting and roll the dough through the machine about four times. Do this by running it through once, folding over and rolling through again; repeat three times. Sprinkle with flour again. Move the setting to the next notch down and run through repeatedly until it is 1 mm thick (roughly 4 times). Your strip should end up being roughly 2 meters long. Fold in half to find the middle, and mark.

Place 1 tablespoonful of squash at even intervals, achieving eight blobs. Paint a strip of water in a square around each blob. Then fold the top sheet over the blobs and press down to glue along your watermark. Push the air gently out from the parcel, otherwise the ravioli will fill up with water while boiling. Cut evenly between the filling

leaving 1 cm of dough from edge to filling. Repeat the process with the second half of the dough.

In a saucepan, large enough for the ravioli to move around while cooking, bring about 4 litres of water to the boil, add 1 teaspoon of salt and when boiling, lower in the ravioli and cook for at least 10 minutes or until they float up to the surface.

Meanwhile wash, drain and dry the rocket. Whisk together the olive oil, walnut oil and red wine vinegar to make a dressing.

Melt the butter in a frying pan, add the sage leaves, pumpkin seeds and lemon juice and sprinkle with salt. Allow the butter to froth; cook for 10-12 minutes. Remove the ravioli parcels with a slotted spoon and place on a serving plate. Pour the butter and sage over plus lots of freshly ground pepper. Serve with rocket salad and walnut dressing.

Walnut & Cheddar Cake with Braised Celery

I love walnuts and I do think it's worth getting hold of them in shells as they taste so much better. We use Haford and Lloyd Green's organic cheddar cheeses at the Duke, but don't feel bound to cheddar, most cheese will work extremely well here.

Ingredients *(serves 4)*

- 500 g mixed root vegetables, peeled and cubed (swede, turnip, celeriac, carrot etc)
- 25 g butter
- 2 tbsp olive oil
- 1 head celery
- 200 ml vegetable stock (page 152)
- 1 clove garlic
- 5 g butter
- Salt and pepper
- 4 cloves garlic, finely chopped
- 1 onion, finely chopped
- 2 sprigs rosemary, finely chopped
- 2 sprigs thyme, finely chopped
- 50 g breadcrumbs
- 75 g shelled walnuts, chopped
- 100 g strong cheddar, grated (or any other strong cheese)
- 1 tbsp parsley, chopped

Method

Preheat the oven to 200C/400F/gas 6.

Place the root vegetables in an oven proof dish with the butter, a tablespoon of oil, a couple of spoons of water and season. Cook for 20 minutes or until soft.

Meanwhile, cut the root off the celery; wash. Pull off any leaves, which can be kept for salad or stock. Cut into 5 cm pieces across. Put aside.

Heat up the vegetable stock. Place the celery in an ovenproof dish and pour over the vegetable stock. Crush 1 clove of garlic, put in with the celery, the butter and seasoning. Cover with foil. Leave in the oven for about 40 minutes; if the celery is very thick leave it for a bit longer.

In a frying pan fry the remaining garlic, onion, rosemary and thyme, with a tablespoon of oil until soft.

When the root vegetables are really soft mash with a potato masher, place in a bowl; add the fried garlic-onion-herb mix, breadcrumbs, the roughly chopped walnuts and half the cheese.

Taste and season. Place in a buttered round tin or shallow dish, line with greaseproof paper if it might leak. Sprinkle the remaining cheddar on top. Cook in the oven for 20 minutes.

Sprinkle the celery with chopped parsley. With a slotted spoon, place the braised celery on the plate and serve with the walnut and cheddar cake.

Roast Pork with Celeriac Mash & Apple Cider Sauce

Use a really good cider for this dish and don't waste your money on poor apples; embrace the wonderful range of British apples. Your pork must be sourced from an excellent farm, as I said on page 50.

Ingredients *(serves 4)*
- 1.5 kg rolled leg or shoulder of pork
- 50 g sea salt
- 1 onion
- 1 carrot
- 3 cloves garlic
- Large sprig rosemary
- Corn or plain flour

Celeriac mash
- 2 medium celeriac
- Pinch of salt
- 4 cloves garlic
- 50 g butter
- 100 ml single cream

Apple sauce
- 400 g cooking apples
- 30 g sugar
- 75 ml cider, plus extra for gravy

Method
Preheat the oven to 240C/475F/gas 9.

Rub the salt into the skin of the joint, pushing in as much as possible to ensure a delicious crackling.

Cut the onion and carrot into thick chunks, coarsely crush the garlic and rosemary then place into a roasting tin.

Heat a frying pan and sear the pork joint on all sides, this will help keep the juices in. Place the pork on top of the vegetables and place in the oven for no more than 30 minutes, then reduce the heat to 190C/375F/gas 5 and cook for a further 1 and a half hours.

While the pork is cooking peel the celeriac and cut into chunks. Place in a saucepan of cold water with some salt and the crushed garlic. Set to one side.

Peel and core the apples and cut into small chunks. Place in a saucepan with the sugar and cider, bring to the boil and simmer till soft. With a hand blender, blend and set to one side.

About 10 minutes before you are due to take out the pork, check the skin; if it hasn't started to blister into crackling, turn up the oven heat until it does. In the meantime bring the celeriac to the boil.

While the celeriac is cooking, and when you are sure that the skin is looking crisp, take the pork out of the oven and place somewhere warm to stand, this allows the juices to settle back into the meat. To check the pork is cooked, the juice should run clear, never pink. (You can cut off the skin and pop it back into the oven to crisp it if you don't want your meat too well done.)

Discard all the vegetables from the pork roasting tin, but keep all the juices. Put the tin over the heat, add a teaspoon of flour, cook, add a dash of cider and cook for a few minutes to make gravy.

When the celeriac is tender – about 20 minutes – drain. Add the butter and cream and mash or whisk till smooth. Season with salt and pepper.

Slice the pork thickly and serve with the celeriac, gravy, apple sauce and a seasonal green vegetable like purple sprouting broccoli.

Carrot & Honey Cake

Well, it has carrots in it, so it has to be more healthy than most puddings, although I really like this one for afternoon tea. Use UK or Fairtrade honey – there are some wonderful ones in London which is one of the easiest places in the UK to produce honey due to the abundance of flowers.

Ingredients *(serves 4)*

- 200 g raw grated carrot
- 175 g butter
- 175 g caster sugar
- 2 tbsp honey
- 3 eggs
- 110 g plain flour
- 110 g self raising flour
- Half heaped tsp baking powder
- 2 tsp mixed spice (or cinnamon, mace, allspice, ginger)
- 1 tsp fresh ground nutmeg
- 100 g sultanas
- Zest of 1 orange

Method

Preheat the oven to 180C/350F/gas 4.

Cream together the butter and sugar. Add the honey. Add one egg at a time, whisking slowly.

Mix together the flours, baking powder and spices.

Fold the flour mix into the creamed butter using a spatula. Add the sultanas, zest of orange and finally the grated carrots. Mix together and place in a buttered 20 cm long x 8 cm deep bread tin. Cook in the oven for about 50 minutes to 1 hour. Test with a skewer in the centre: it should come out clean.

Serve with whipped cream or icing sugar.

Port Stewed Damsons & Blackberries with Vanilla Shortbread

Quintessential British fruits, damsons and blackberries, and stewing in port with shortbread couldn't celebrate that more. Double the shortbread mix to keep some for the next day or two.

Ingredients *(serves 4)*

- Zest of 1 lemon
- Half vanilla pod, seeds scraped out
- 200 g plain flour
- 12 damsons, washed
- 200 g blackberries, washed
- 50 g raw cane sugar
- 1 cinnamon stick (3 cm long)
- 100 ml port
- 50 ml water

Shortbread

- 125 g butter at room temperature
- 100 g caster sugar
- 300 g plain flour

Method

Preheat the oven to 200C/400F/gas 6.

Place the shortbread ingredients in a mixing bowl and combine with a wooden spoon. Finish with your fingertips, making sure there are no lumps of butter.

Mould the mix into a sausage shape about 10 cm long, wrap in clingfilm and leave to rest in the fridge for 20 minutes. Take the mix out of the fridge, slice into 0.5 cm slices, and place on a parchment paper-covered baking tray. Bake in the oven for about 10-12 minutes or until light golden brown.

Cut the damsons in half lengthwise (down either side of the stone). Put them in a saucepan with the blackberries. Add the sugar, cinnamon stick, port and water. Let simmer on a low heat for about five minutes or until the damsons are a bit soft but still hold their shape. Place in serving bowls with the liquid and serve with the shortbread.

Cardamom Poached Pears with Biscotti

We have many fine varieties of pear so do hunt one out for this dish. The cardamom and cinnamon make this a warming dish for a chilling autumnal day. The biscotti will keep for a week in an airtight container, so we have made a mix enough for 20.

Ingredients *(serves 4)*
- 4 ripe pears
- 500 ml sweet red wine (or red wine with 50 g more sugar)
- 50 g raw cane sugar
- 2 green cardamom pods, crushed
- 1 bay leaf
- 1 x 3 cm cinnamon stick
- 1 star anise
- 2 cloves
- Juice of half a lemon
- 200 ml water

Biscotti
- 250 g plain flour
- 250 g caster sugar
- Half tsp baking powder
- 2 eggs
- 1 egg yolk
- 1 tsp cardamom seeds or fennel seeds or pistachios or almonds

Vanilla cream
- 200 ml double cream
- 1 tsp vanilla extract

Method

Preheat the oven to 180C/350F/gas 4. To make the biscotti place all the ingredients in a food processor. Blend until the mix comes together, the consistency is very sticky. Cover a baking tray with baking paper, and dollop the whole mixture in the middle of the sheet, so it forms a long oval shape about 2 cm thick. Bake in the oven for 30 minutes. Reduce the oven temperature to 120C/250F/gas ½.

Remove the biscotti from the oven, put on a chopping board, and slice with bread knife into 0.5 cm slices. Return the slices to the baking tray, and bake for a further 30 minutes. Turn them over and bake for a further 30 minutes. Place them to cool on a cooling rack.

Peel the pears, leaving the stalks and tails on, do this as neatly as possible. Place the wine, sugar and spices but not the pears in a saucepan. Bring to the boil and then place the pears in the wine syrup and simmer with a lid on for about 20 minutes or until soft. Half way through cooking, turn over. Put a knife into the pears to test if cooked; it should go in easily but the pears should still be a bit firm.

To make the vanilla cream place the cream and vanilla extract in a bowl and whisk until it peaks.

Serve one pear per person by placing a pear in a wide soup bowl with a bit of the wine syrup and a dollop of cream on each one and biscotti on the side.

Moist Chocolate and Almond Cake

A very simple but rich and satisfying cake which can be served warm or cold. Fairtrade chocolate is a must and it is very easy to get hold of excellent quality these days.

Ingredients *(serves 6-8)*

- ~ 8 eggs
- ~ 330 g caster sugar
- ~ 350 g dark chocolate
- ~ 50 g plain flour
- ~ 50 g ground almonds
- ~ 210 g butter
- ~ 1 tsp vanilla essence
- ~ 100 ml water

Method

Preheat the oven to 160C/325F/gas 3.

Whisk the eggs and sugar together until pale and fluffy, then set aside.

Chop the chocolate as finely as you can, and place in a bowl. Add the flour and ground almonds and set aside.

Place the butter, vanilla essence and water in a pot, bring to the boil, pour this over the chocolate mix. Whisk until all the chocolate melts, let it cool then fold into the egg mixture.

Do ensure you fold, as it's very important to keep in as many air bubbles as possible.

Butter a 22 cm cake tin and pour in the mix.

Place in the preheated oven for 40 minutes. Insert a knife into the middle to ensure it's cooked, it should come out clean. Serve with whipped cream or crème fraîche.

DUKE COOK BOOK - WINTER

STARTERS
* POTTED SMOKED HORSERADISH MACKEREL
* SPICED BROWN LENTIL SOUP W/ YOGHURT
* BLUE CHEESE, ROCKET, PEAR + WALNUT SALAD
* GRILLED SARDINES W/ GREMOLATA
* BRAISED PIGS CHEEKS ON TOAST
* CREAM OF OXTAIL + PEARL BARLEY BROTH

MAINS
* COCKLE, COLEY + GURNARD FISH STEW W/ CROSTINI + SAFFRON GARLIC MAYONNAISE
* OAT CRUSTED HERRING W/ PARSNIP CHIPS + MUSHY PEAS
* VENISON STEAK W/ SWEDE + CELERIAC ROSTI, CHARD + PORT GRAVY
* ROAST PHEASANT W/ POTATO + STILTON GRATIN + CAVOLO NERO
* PIGEON W/ ROAST SQUASH, BRUSSEL SPROUTS + PRUNES
* CARAMELISED ONION + STILTON TARTLETS W/ HONEY ROAST ROOT VEGETABLES
* POTATO + SPINACH GNOCCHI
* CELERIAC, POTATO + STICHELTON CAKE W/ SPINACH, BEETROOT + BALSAMIC
* SEA BASS W/ ROAST BEETROOT, GREEN LENTILS + BACON + HORSERADISH CREAM

PUDDINGS
* RICE PUDDING W/ DRIED FRUIT COMPOTE
* CHOCOLATE + HAZELNUT TORTE
* APPLE, WALNUT + CINNAMON SPONGE CAKE W/ CREME ANGLAISE
* BEETROOT + FRUIT CAKE W/ LEMON ICING

1. WE ARE THE UK'S FIRST-AND-ONLY GASTROPUB WITH ORGANIC CERTIFICATI FROM THE SOIL ASSOCIATION

2. 80% OF OUR FRESH PRODUCE COMES F THE HOME COUNTIES AND OUR BEER IS BREWED CLOSE TO LONDON. WE KEEP OUR FOOD MILES EXTREMELY LOW, AND NEVER AIRFREIG

3. EVERYTHING WE SELL IS ORGANIC* FROM O HOME BAKED BREAD TO OUR HOMEMADE ICECREAM + PICKLES. OUR FOOD EXCEPTIONAL PURITY + QUALITY.

4. WE CHANGE OUR MENU DAILY ACCORDING WHAT'S AVAILABLE - IF SOMETHING ISN'T IN SEASON, YOU FIND IT ON THE MENU

5. OUR FISH BUYING POLICY IS APPROVED BY MARINE CONSERVATION SOCIETY AND WE SOURCE FRO SUSTAINABLE MARINE STEWARDSHIP COUNCIL CERTIFIED FISH WHEREVER POSSIBLE. ALL OUR FISH IS CAUGHT ACCORDING TO SUSTAIN SMALL DAY BOATS OFF THE SOUTH WEST COAST.

6. YOU'LL FIND LESSER KNOWN FISH SPECIES THE MENU - SUCH AS THE ENDANGERED BALOCK, GURNARD CLAMS. ALL OUR PURCHASING IS STRICTLY MONITORED

7. ALL OUR MEAT COMES FROM SMALL LOCAL FARMS WHERE THE HIGHEST LEVELS OF ANIMAL WELFARE EMPLOYED. WE NEVER, EVER BATTERY - FOR EXAMPLE OUR CHICKS BUY A WHOLE AND WE USE EVERY PART OF THE ANIMAL.

8. WE ARE OBSESSED WITH HAVING THE EST CARBON FOOTPRINT POSSIBLE WHEREVER POSSIBLE, AND OUR ELECTRICITY IS

ELEBRATE TEN YEAR AINABLE BUSINESS OUR VALUABLE SUPPORT.

MAY BE CERTIFIED AS ORG LEGAL - QUALITY GUIDELIN

OLICY WHICH HAS BEEN C UNCIL'S ENVIRONMENTAL RE FISHERY. WWW.MSC.

Winter

Starters

Potted Smoked Horseradish Mackerel

Spiced Brown Lentil Soup with Yoghurt

Blue Cheese, Rocket, Pear & Walnut Salad

Grilled Sardines with Gremolata

Braised Pigs' Cheeks on Toast

Cream of Oxtail & Pearl Barley Broth

Mains

Cockle, Coley and Gurnard Fish Stew with Crostini & Saffron Garlic Mayo

Oat-crusted Herring with Parsnip Chips & Mushy Peas

Venison Steak with Swede & Celeriac Rosti, Chard & Port Gravy

Roast Pheasant, Potato & Stilton Gratin & Cavolo Nero

Pigeon with Roast Squash, Brussels Sprouts & Prunes

Caramelised Onion & Stilton Tartlets with Honey Roast Root Vegetables

Potato & Spinach Gnocchi

Celeriac, Potato and Stichelton Cake with Spinach, Beetroot & Balsamic

Sea Bass, Roast Beetroot, Green Lentil & Bacon with Horseradish Cream

Puddings

Rice Pudding with Dried Fruit Compote

Chocolate & Hazelnut Torte

Apple, Walnut & Cinnamon Sponge Cake with Crème Anglaise

Beetroot Fruit Cake with Lemon Icing

BRITISH SEASONAL VEGETABLES
WINTER

APPLES
ASIAN GREENS
PURPLE SPROUTING BROCCOLI
BRUSSELS SPROUTS
CABBAGE
CARROTS
CAULIFLOWER
CELERIAC
HERBS - PERENNIAL
JERUSALEM ARTICHOKES
KALE

LEEKS
MUSHROOMS
PARSNIPS
RHUBARB
SHALLOTS
SPINACH
SPRING ONIONS
SPRING GREENS
SWEDE
WINTER SQUASH

THIS IS A LIST OF SEASONAL VEGETABLES
WHEN THE PRODUCE IS LIKELY TO BE AT ITS BEST

Geetie & Mabel

Potted Smoked Horseradish Mackerel

You can keep this dish for at least a week in the fridge if well sealed. Either serve it in individual dishes or one big one. And of course, there are all sorts of variations by adding herbs like parsley, chives or tarragon.

Ingredients *(serves 6)*

- 150 g butter (leave some to put on top of the pot)
- 500 g flaked, smoked mackerel
- 50 g grated fresh horseradish, or 6 tsp from a jar
- Juice half a lemon
- Fresh ground black pepper
- Toast / gherkins / capers to serve
- 1 lemon to serve

Method

To clarify the butter place it in a pan and slowly heat until melted and the milk solids (whey and salt) come to the top. Spoon off this white substance and discard.

Put the smoked mackerel in a large bowl, mash with a wooden spoon and a fork if needed. Slowly add two thirds of the clarified butter, and mix in thoroughly with a wooden spoon, the mackerel will be soft enough for it to get pretty light.

Add grated horseradish, lemon juice and season with plenty of fresh ground black pepper.

Taste. The mackerel should make it salty enough not to need salt.

Press the smoked mackerel down into a small pot and cover with the rest of the clarified butter. Put in the fridge for a few hours, and take out 15 minutes before eating. Serve with toast, gherkins and capers, or your own pickled cucumber (page 146) or beetroot (page 144) and quarters of lemon.

Spiced Brown Lentil Soup with Yoghurt

Lentils and dried beans become a staple of the winter diet when eating seasonally. I think they are absolutely delicious with so many ways of using them. This is a warming wholesome meal or starter.

Ingredients *(serves 4)*

- ~ 5 g butter
- ~ 2 tsp oil
- ~ 2 carrots, scrubbed and finely chopped
- ~ 1 onion, finely chopped
- ~ 2 sticks celery, finely chopped
- ~ 4 cloves garlic, finely sliced
- ~ 1 tsp chilli powder
- ~ 2 tsp coriander seeds
- ~ 2 tsp caraway seeds
- ~ 2 tsp cumin seeds
- ~ 200 g brown lentils
- ~ 500 ml stock (meat or vegetable, page 152)
- ~ Salt and pepper, to taste
- ~ 2 tbsp natural yoghurt, to serve (page 149)

Method

Heat the butter and oil in a saucepan and gently fry the vegetables and chilli powder until soft.

Dry roast the coriander, caraway and cumin seeds in a frying pan for a few minutes until golden brown. Grind them finely in a pestle and mortar and add to the vegetables with the brown lentils and stir.

Pour in the stock. Allow to simmer for about 30 minutes.

Add salt and black pepper to taste, and chilli sauce if you prefer it hotter. Add more stock or water if the soup is too thick.

Serve with a big dollop of yoghurt.

Blue Cheese, Rocket, Pear & Walnut Salad

This really is a delightful salad, the rocket cuts through the blue cheese and is offset by the sweetness of the pear and walnut. Stichelton is a wonderful blue cheese from Neal's Yard which I highly recommend, but of course there are many other excellent blue cheeses if you prefer.

Ingredients *(serves 4)*

- ~ Pinch of salt
- ~ 1 clove garlic
- ~ 1 tbsp Dijon mustard
- ~ 2 tbsp red wine vinegar
- ~ 200 ml olive oil
- ~ 80 g walnuts, in their shells
- ~ Half tsp sugar
- ~ 1 pear
- ~ 400 g rocket, washed and dried
- ~ 100 g Stichelton or other blue cheese

Method

Using a pestle and mortar, grind the salt and garlic and then add the mustard and red wine vinegar. Mix them, and slowly add the olive oil.

Shell the walnuts and place in a roasting tray with a sprinkle of sugar and salt. Grill or roast for about 5 minutes making sure you turn regularly, until golden brown.

Core and slice the pear. Place in a mixing bowl with the dressing and rocket, turning to coat the leaves and pear.

Serve on to plates, sprinkle with the walnuts and finally add big chunks of cheese.

Grilled Sardines with Gremolata

Pilchards were their old name, but they are now known as the Cornish sardine, and stocks are very healthy. I remember them in cans when I was a kid, in a tomato sauce. Mum would give them to us for lunch in sandwiches, I think she mixed them with a dressing and I remember rather liking them. But these days the Cornish sardine is regarded as a more sophisticated lunch. Served as they are here they are light and aromatic.

Ingredients *(serves 4)*
- 2 sardines per portion, or 3 for a main course
- Salt and pepper
- 1 tbsp olive oil

Gremolata
- 100 g flat leaf parsley
- 1 lemon
- 1 clove garlic
- 2 lemons, cut in half, to serve

Method
To make the gremolata finely chop the parsley, place in a mixing bowl and then grate the lemon on the finer side of a grater. Make sure you don't use any of the (white) pith of the lemon, only the rind. Finely chop the garlic. Mix well together.

Season the sardines and drizzle with olive oil. Place on a really hot grill or in a frying pan. Put the lemon on the grill as well, to mark. Cook the fish for roughly 4 minutes on each side until the flesh is cooked through.

Serve with the gremolata and grilled lemon, and drizzle with olive oil.

Braised Pigs' Cheeks on Toast

You don't see pigs' cheeks on many restaurant menus, but they are a really superb bit of the beast. It's absolutely essential that we use the whole animal in our quest for a greener, leaner planet, and this dish embraces that.

Ingredients *(serves 4 as a starter or 2 as a main course)*
- *2 pig's cheeks per person (so 8) as starter, or 4 per person as main course*
- *2 sticks celery*
- *4 small onions*
- *2 carrots (can add more root vegetables and mushrooms)*
- *6 cloves garlic*
- *1 chilli*
- *2 tbsp olive oil*
- *2 bay leaves*
- *1 litre red wine*
- *3 tbsp balsamic vinegar*
- *1 litre meat stock (page 152)*
- *2 handfuls of cress – (you can grow this at home on your window sill all year round)*
- *Bread, for toast*

Method
Drain the pigs' cheeks of any blood.

Cut the vegetables into equal 1 cm cubes. Finely chop the garlic and chilli.

Place a saucepan on medium heat, add a spoon of oil and fry the vegetables and bay leaves. Meanwhile heat a frying pan to really hot, add oil and fry the pigs' cheeks on each side until golden brown. Add to the vegetables. Now add the red wine and balsamic vinegar and allow to reduce for 5 minutes on a high heat. Lower the heat, add the meat stock and let it simmer for about an hour and a half until the cheeks are soft.

Season with salt and freshly ground pepper. Serve on toast with cress on top.

Cream of Oxtail & Pearl Barley Broth

Oxtail soup is a well known dish that is rarely cooked these days, which is a terrible shame as it's wonderfully tasty and incorporates head to toe eating. Cooking and serving the meat on the bone adds flavour and a bit of extra work when you are eating it, slowing down the pleasure of consuming it.

Ingredients *(serves 4)*
- *4 chunks of oxtail, roughly 80 g each*
- *1 tbsp flour, seasoned*
- *2 tbsp sunflower oil*
- *2 sticks celery, sliced*
- *2 carrots, finely chopped*
- *Half swede, finely chopped*
- *3 cloves garlic, finely chopped*
- *200 g pearl barely, rinsed*
- *1 litre meat stock (page 152)*
- *100 ml single cream*

Method
Start by coating the oxtail in the seasoned flour. Get a saucepan really hot, add the oil and sear the oxtail pieces.

Take the oxtail out but leave the pan on the heat. Add the chopped vegetables to the pan and fry until golden brown. Put the oxtail on top of the vegetables, then the barley. Cover with the meat stock and let it simmer for an hour and a half. Taste and season. Just before you are due to serve, stir in the cream.

Cockle, Coley and Gurnard Fish Stew with Crostini & Saffron Garlic Mayo

The choice of fish you use in this recipe is entirely up to you, but probably not a heavy oily fish like mackerel. You can use any shellfish really, clams and mussels will be the most sustainable and are a great alternative to prawns. Prawns are better avoided altogether as the industry commits some shocking atrocities. Certainly never ever buy a prawn that doesn't have MSC assurances attached to it.

We have used cockles here. When I was a child, I remember my uncle eating them in pubs, pickled in jars. The Bury Inlet fishery in South Wales is certified by the MSC, so the most perfect place to get them from if you can. They should be eaten in the autumn or winter, and from licensed hand gatherers if they're not MSC certified.

Ingredients *(serves 4)*

Mayonnaise
- Juice of half a lemon
- Pinch of saffron
- 2 cloves garlic
- Pinch of sea salt
- 2 egg yolks
- 1 tsp Dijon mustard
- 2 tsp white wine vinegar
- Olive oil
- Salt and pepper

Fish stew
- 4 cloves garlic, finely chopped
- 1 onion, finely chopped
- 3 sticks celery, finely chopped
- 2 small leeks, sliced finely
- 1 x 240 g tin tomatoes
- 200 ml white wine
- 200 ml fish stock (page 153)
- 200 g coley
- 200 g fillet of gurnard
- 24 cockles (or 12 mussels)

To serve
- Toasted thinly sliced bread, for crostini

Method

Place the lemon juice and the saffron in a saucepan and simmer until it's infused. In a pestle and mortar crush the garlic with sea salt. Place the egg yolks, Dijon mustard and wine vinegar and garlic in a bowl and blend it with a hand blender, then slowly add the olive oil until thick, add the lemon juice and saffron and continue whisking, adding more oil if needed.

Heat oil in a saucepan, add the vegetables and fry until soft. Add the tinned tomatoes and the white wine, simmer and reduce. Add the fish stock and let simmer for about 15 minutes. Lastly add the fish and season, cover with a lid and serve within 5 minutes. Discard any unopened cockles.

Serve the fish stew hot in bowls. Spread the mayo on the crostini and float it on top of the stew.

Oat-crusted Herring with Parsnip Chips & Mushy Peas

The story of herring is one of the few fishing industry successes in recent years. In the 70's stocks were near collapse in the UK. We then had a total ban on their harvest. In its absence, the knock-on effect was to spoil our appetite for the tasty oily fish which has meant it has stayed off our plates ever since.

These days stocks have recovered, but not to their original quantities, because of being undermined by modern fishing methods. We do need to ensure that, as always, we buy from sustainable sources or we could easily send stock levels sliding back to the lows of the 70's. There are a couple of MSC-certified fisheries for herring, which is the best place to be buying from. We buy from the MSC Hastings and Thames Blackwater fisheries.

Ingredients *(serves 4)*

- 200 g green split peas
- 1 bay leaf
- 1 clove garlic
- 5 g butter
- Juice of 1 lemon
- 1 tbsp fresh mint if possible, if not, dried
- 600 g parsnips, peeled if the skin is tough
- 2 whole herring per person, gutted and scaled
- 4 whole eggs
- 100 g oats
- Oil to fry
- Salt and pepper

Method

Rinse the green split peas under cold water in a colander. Place 1 litre of water in a saucepan, add the bay leaf, garlic and the green split peas and a pinch of salt. Let simmer for about 30 minutes or until soft. Drain the excess water off and smash the peas with a potato masher, you want to keep some bean texture. Then add salt and pepper, a knob of butter, the juice of a lemon, and some mint if you have any.

While the peas are cooking, cut the parsnips into 1 cm x 4 cm chips, bring a pan of water to the boil, and simmer the parsnips for 2-3 minutes. They should be quite al dente; drain and fry gently with the butter, salt and pepper for 10-15 minutes, shaking the pan every now and again till they crisp.

While the parsnips are cooking, put the beaten eggs on a large plate or a tray, then do the same with oats. Dip the herrings into the egg and then the oats. Heat a frying pan, add a little oil, and fry the herrings until golden brown on each side for 5-7 minutes. Add a knob of butter to the pan a couple of minutes before you serve.

Serve the mushy peas, with the herring and chips on the side and a wedge of lemon.

Venison Steak with Swede & Celeriac Rosti, Chard & Port Gravy

Venison is a succulent and tasty meat which goes down a treat in the pub and especially with my nephew Floyd! When buying venison ensure that it is wild. Wild deer can be an awful pest in some parts of the county doing terrible damage to crops and trees, so eating the wild version can only be of benefit to the countryside. What we mustn't allow to happen is for them to be culled and not eaten. The next best places to buy from are country estates where they wouldn't be producing much else in the way of food on their land.

Ingredients *(serves 4)*

- 4 venison steaks, 200 g each; or 1 kg fillet of venison cut into 4 steaks
- 100 ml port
- 100 ml meat stock *(page 152)*

Rosti

- 250 g swede
- 250 g celeriac
- 1 onion, finely sliced
- 2 tbsp plain flour
- Knob of butter

- 1 kg chard
- 5 g butter

Method

Wash, peel and grate the swede and celeriac and place in a bowl. Add the sliced onion and flour, season with salt and pepper, and mix. Shape into 4 little flat cakes or patties.

Heat a frying pan to medium heat, add the butter and fry the rosties. Brown both sides and cook on a low heat for about 7 minutes each side.

While the patties are cooking, get a frying pan really hot, place the seasoned venison steaks into the pan, and sear all sides for about 3 minutes each side. Remove the steaks from the frying pan, and place on a plate, cover with foil and leave to rest. Keeping the frying pan on the heat, put the port into it and let this boil until reduced by half. Add meat stock and let simmer for a few minutes. Add any meat juices from the venison steaks to the gravy.

Remove any tough stalks of the chard, heat up a pan, add the butter and cook the chard for roughly 2-3 minutes until cooked.

Serve immediately.

Roast Pheasant, Potato & Stilton Gratin & Cavolo Nero

Game is a very sustainable form of meat. Make sure you ask your butcher for wild pheasant, not the sort you usually get which are released and shot 'in total carnage' in the words of Todd, from Food for Thought, who supplies the pub with ours.

Ingredients (serves 4)
Preparation: 1-5 hours marinade
- 2 pheasants, cut into halves
- 25 g rosemary
- 25 g thyme
- 3 cloves garlic
- 1 tbsp olive oil

Gratin
- 200 ml cream
- 4 sprigs thyme, chopped
- Half onion, sliced
- 1 clove garlic, crushed
- 800 g potatoes
- 50 g stilton
- 400 g cavolo nero
- 75 g butter
- 1 tbsp balsamic vinegar
- Salt and pepper

Method

Chop the rosemary, thyme and garlic, and mix with the olive oil and rub into the pheasant halves. Place in the fridge for at least an hour, but 5 hours would be best.

Preheat the oven to 200C/400F/gas 6.

To make the gratin put the cream, chopped thyme, onion and garlic in a saucepan and cook together until well infused – at least 10 minutes. Season.

Scrub the potatoes and slice them thinly. Use a knob of the butter to grease an ovenproof dish. Place a layer of potatoes and crumble a bit of stilton over them, continue layering the potatoes and stilton finishing with potatoes. Strain the onion, garlic and thyme from the cream and pour over the gratin.

Cover with a lid or foil and place in the oven. Make sure you have a large tray underneath, as there may be drips. Cook for about 40 minutes or until done, test by inserting a knife in the middle – it should feel soft.

While the gratin is cooking put the pheasant halves in a heated frying pan and colour their skins all over. Put this in the oven too for about 15 minutes. Take out and rest them for 10 minutes before serving.

Strip the tough stalks off the cavolo nero, heat the remaining butter in a pan and toss the cavolo for 2-3 minutes or until cooked. Serve half a pheasant per person on a plate with a slice of gratin, some cavolo nero and drizzle with balsamic vinegar.

Pigeon with Roast Squash, Brussels Sprouts & Prunes

Pigeon may not be easy to get from all butchers, but it's a really lovely meat so well worth the effort of hunting some out. It is also classed as vermin, so some, like farmers who have to defend their crops from it, will be glad you are eating it.

Ingredients *(serves 4)*
- 4 whole pigeons, plucked
- Salt and black pepper
- 2 carrots, scrubbed and roughly chopped
- 2 cloves garlic, crushed
- 1 onion, roughly chopped
- 4 sprigs thyme
- 50 g butter
- 1 squash, peeled and cut into 1 cm cubes
- 3 cloves garlic, crushed
- 2 tsp olive oil
- 50 g butter
- 400 g Brussels sprouts, tailed and outer leaves removed as needed
- 50 g butter
- 100 ml red wine
- 200 ml meat stock (page 152)
- 200 g ready-to-eat prunes

Method
Preheat the oven to 220C/425F/gas 7.

Clean the pigeons by removing the heart and livers (you can ask your butcher to do this) and wash under the tap. Season with salt and pepper inside and out.

Heat a large frying pan and sear the pigeons on all sides.

Put the carrots, garlic cloves and onion in a roasting tin, lay the pigeons on top, adding the sprigs of thyme and the butter. Place in the oven and cook for 15 minutes.

Meanwhile, put the cubes of squash, 3 cloves of crushed garlic, oil and salt and pepper in another roasting tray with butter in the oven for about 15 minutes or until soft.

Put a pan of water on for the Brussels sprouts, when the water is boiling, add the sprouts and cook for 5 minutes. Toss in butter and season.

Remove the pigeons from the oven and leave them to rest for roughly 10 minutes in a warm place.

Place the roasting tray on the stove, add the red wine, reduce rapidly, add the meat stock and boil for a further 5 minutes. Strain, discarding the vegetables, and keeping the liquid add the prunes and any juices from the pigeon, reduce further if needed, you want it down to roughly a third.

Serve the pigeon with the roast squash, Brussels sprouts and prune gravy.

Caramelised Onion & Stilton Tartlets with Honey Roast Root Vegetables

These are great as individual tarts, but can just as easily be made as one big one. You don't have to stick to stilton or blue cheese of course, you can use any strong cheese. Or, with households in the UK wasting a third of the food we buy, just use up all those leftover chunks of cheese you have.

Ingredients *(serves 4)*
- Pastry (page 148)
- 50 g butter
- 2 tbsp sunflower oil
- 3 large onions, finely sliced
- 2 cloves garlic, finely chopped
- 6 sprigs thyme, finely chopped
- 100 ml double cream
- 2 whole eggs
- 3 egg yolks, plus 1 yolk for glazing the pastry
- Seasoning
- 50 g Stilton or other blue or strong cheese, sliced
- 200 g parsnips, peeled
- 200 g carrots, peeled
- 200-300 g pumpkin, peeled
- 2 tbsp olive oil
- 10 g butter
- 2 tbsp runny honey

To cook
- 4 x 12 cm tartlet tins

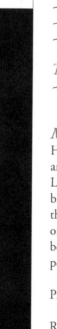

Method
Heat a saucepan to medium heat, add the butter and oil, and put in the onions, garlic and thyme. Lower the heat and allow to cook until golden brown, which will take about 40 minutes. Stir so that it doesn't stick. The longer you leave the onions cooking the sweeter and tastier they will be. Season with salt and freshly ground black pepper.

Preheat the oven to 180C/350F/gas 4.

Roll out the pastry on a floured surface. Fill the individual tartlet tins with pastry and gently fork holes in the bottom to prevent the base bubbling when blind baking. Place in the oven for 30-40 minutes. Remove from the oven and glaze with one beaten egg yolk. Allow to cool.

Whisk the cream, whole eggs and yolks until blended, fold in the cooked onions. Season. Place the onion mix into the tartlets and put sliced Stilton on the top.

Bake in the oven at 200C/400F/gas 6 for about 20 minutes or until set.

While the tarts are cooking, prepare the vegetables – cut the parsnip, carrot and pumpkin into 2 cm pieces. Place on a baking tray, drizzle with olive oil and add the butter. Put in the oven for 15 minutes, take out, drizzle with honey and cook for a further 5 minutes or until done.

Serve while hot along with the tartlets.

Potato & Spinach Gnocchi

Lots of people are dismissive of gnocchi, but that's only because they have had it badly made. It can take a little practice to get it just how you like it, but it's truly scrummy when it's done right – light and melting in your mouth.

I love this version of Sara's and of course it can be eaten all year round with variations – plain potato or pumpkin in winter, nettle or wild garlic in spring or just herb based. Cheese of most sorts will complement too.

Ingredients *(serves 4)*
- *1 kg floury potatoes, of equal size*
- *100 g butter*
- *Half tsp salt*
- *1 tsp nutmeg*
- *200 g spinach*
- *250 g plain flour*
- *200 g hard goat's cheese – grated (or other good quality tasty hard cheese)*
- *Lots of pepper*

Method
Scrub the potatoes and place, whole, in a saucepan, cover with water, add a pinch of salt and cook for half an hour or until cooked. It's important to leave the potatoes whole so they don't take in too much water and with this in mind, don't over cook them, better slightly under done.

While the potatoes cook, melt half the butter, add salt and nutmeg and fry the spinach until it's wilted. When it's cooled, with your hands, squeeze out and discard the liquid.

When the potatoes are cooked, mash, add the flour and spinach and mix well with your hands. (You can peel the potatoes if you prefer, but I think the skins add flavour and create less waste.) This should be a dry mixture, so it's no longer sticking to the sides of the bowl. Add more flour if required. Taste and season as needed, be generous.

Divide the mix into 2 halves and on a well floured surface, roll out into sausages of roughly 2 cm thick. Cut the sausages into 2 cm pieces. You can gently shape into oblongs with your hands if you wish, but I like the random squares.

Bring a big pan of salted water to a rapid boil. Drop the gnocchi into the water and cook for about 3 minutes, or until they rise to the surface. Remove with a draining spoon.

Heat the remaining butter in a large frying pan till bubbling and starting to brown. Add the gnocchi and fry till lightly browned on both sides.

Dish up on warm plates, drizzle with a good olive oil, and sprinkle your cheese on top.

Celeriac, Potato and Stichelton Cake with Spinach, Beetroot & Balsamic

These yummy cakes are a brilliant leftovers dish, using any root vegetable or other cheeses that need finishing up.

Ingredients *(serves 4)*
- 2 large floury potatoes, cut into chunks
- 2 small celeriac, peeled and cut into chunks
- 200 g beetroot
- 1 tbsp honey
- 1 red onion, finely chopped
- 70 g plain flour
- 25 g fresh rosemary, chopped
- 150 g Stichelton, crumbled
- 100 g Parmesan
- 1 tbsp balsamic vinegar
- 200 g spinach
- 1 tbsp olive oil
- 5 g butter

Method

Put the potatoes and celeriac in a saucepan, cover with lightly salted water. Bring to the boil and cook for 20 minutes or until soft – not too soft though.

In the meantime, scrub and top and tail the beetroot and place, whole, in a saucepan. Cover with water, add the honey and a pinch of salt. Boil for 20 minutes. Drain and leave in the pan with a lid on.

When the celeriac and potatoes are ready, mash them coarsely and add the flour. Mix in the onion, rosemary and cheeses, taste and season.

Shape into 4 even cakes. This is best done by making a roughly even layer in the bottom of the pan and then dividing it into 4. Place in the fridge for at least 10 minutes.

Heat up a large frying pan, add oil and turn down the heat, place the cakes in carefully and fry slowly on both sides.

Peel the beetroot and cut into wedges. Place in a saucepan with a knob of butter and toss. Splash some balsamic vinegar into the pan and toss further for a few minutes.

Serve with wilted spinach – spinach sweated down with butter in a pan – season to taste. Also you could serve this dish with your sweet home-made onion marmalade (page 144) that you made with the first onions in summer.

Sea Bass, Roast Beetroot, Green Lentil & Bacon with Horseradish Cream

Choose sea bass which has been sustainably caught by hand-lining methods in the South West of England and enjoy this succulent fleshy fish set off by the bacon and horseradish.

Ingredients *(serves 4)*

- 2 whole large sea bass scaled, filleted and pin boned (ask your fishmonger to do this)
- 400 g beetroot
- 2 tbsp sunflower oil
- 10 g butter
- 1 large onion, finely chopped
- 2 carrots, finely chopped
- 2 cloves garlic, finely chopped
- 200 g smoked bacon, finely chopped
- 250 g green lentils
- 150 ml dry white wine
- 800 ml meat stock (page 152)
- 3 tbsp crème fraîche
- 10 g fresh finely grated horseradish, or 3 tsp from jar
- 3 tsp Dijon mustard, or English mustard, if prefered

Method

Wash the beetroot and place in a saucepan, cover with water and let boil for 20-30 minutes until cooked. Length of time will depend on size. Drain and peel.

Cook the onion, carrots, garlic and bacon gently in a saucepan with 1 tablespoon of sunflower oil and 5 g of butter, but don't allow to brown. Add the green lentils and the white wine, turn up the heat, and allow to reduce until the pan is nearly dry. Add the meat stock and simmer for about 20 minutes. Season.

Meanwhile, mix the crème fraîche with the horseradish and mustard, season, and taste.

Add the last tablespoon of oil to a hot frying pan, season the fish and place, skin side down in the pan and fry for about 3 minutes on one side. Turn the heat down, and push the fish down with a fish slice. Cut the beetroot into wedges, turn over the fish and add the beetroot to the pan, cook for another three minutes. Add the remaining butter to the beetroot and fish. Place the lentils and bacon in a serving dish, scatter the beetroot around and place fish on top with a large dollop of horseradish cream.

Put the extra cream on the table for people to help themselves.

Rice Pudding with Dried Fruit Compote

Rice pudding is not only simple to make, it is yummy comfort food. Dried fruit is the saving grace of seasonal eating, buy Fairtrade whenever you can.

Ingredients – Rice Pudding *(serves 6)*
- ~ *120 g short grain pudding rice*
- ~ *300 ml double cream*
- ~ *300 ml milk*
- ~ *1 cinnamon stick*
- ~ *3 cloves*
- ~ *2 green cardamom pods*
- ~ *2 tsp sugar or to taste*

Method
Wash the rice a few times and drain. Place in a saucepan, add the cream, milk, cinnamon, cloves, cardamom and sugar, and let simmer on a low heat, for 20 minutes. Stir with a spatula occasionally to ensure it doesn't stick. We have added less sugar at this stage as you can always add more at the end to your taste.

Ingredients – Dried Fruit Compote
- ~ *25 g apricots*
- ~ *25 g sultanas and/or raisins*
- ~ *25 g figs*
- ~ *25 g cranberries*
- ~ *1 cinnamon stick*
- ~ *100 ml water*

Method
Slice the fruit into strips. Place all the ingredients in a saucepan and let simmer on a low heat until thick, 15-20 minutes.

Dish the rice pudding up into 6 bowls with a big dollop of fruit compote on top.

The fruit compote has no sugar in it as it's full of sugary fruits.

Chocolate & Hazelnut Torte

Rich and filling, eat for pudding or afternoon tea, but make sure to use Fairtrade dark chocolate.

Ingredients *(serves 6)*
- ~ *125 g shelled hazelnuts*
- ~ *125 g Fairtrade dark chocolate, 70% minimum cocoa*
- ~ *125 g unsalted butter, room temperature*
- ~ *125 g caster sugar*
- ~ *3 eggs*

Method
Preheat the oven to 180C/350F/gas 4.

Roast the hazelnuts in the oven until the skin becomes crisp and the nuts golden brown, about 10 minutes, shaking the roasting tray after 5 minutes.

Place the hot nuts in a tea towel and rub together till all the skin comes off. Put the skinned nuts in a blender and briefly blend to a rough texture.

Take a bowl that will fit over one of your saucepans. Fill the saucepan to a quarter full of water, bring to the boil and turn down to a simmer.

Break the chocolate into small pieces, put in the bowl and place over the saucepan of simmering water. Allow the chocolate to melt slowly.

Whip the soft butter with the sugar until light and fluffy. Slowly whisk in the melted chocolate. Whisk in the eggs one by one. Fold in the crushed nuts. Pour into a lined 22 cm cake tin and bake for 40-50 minutes. To test if it is cooked spike with a knife, it should come out clean. Turn off the oven and leave the torte inside for a further 30 minutes with the door ajar.

Apple, Walnut & Cinnamon Sponge Cake with Crème Anglaise

Fresh walnuts will always taste so much better than ones in packs, but packet ones will of course work just as well. Don't forget to buy local British apples, they need your support.

Ingredients *(serves 6-8)*

- ~ 6 eggs
- ~ 125 g caster sugar
- ~ 300 g flour
- ~ 1 tsp baking powder
- ~ 2 tsp ground cinnamon (keep a few pinches for the top)
- ~ 40 g fresh walnuts, cracked and roughly chopped
- ~ 350 g apples
- ~ 1 tbsp sugar

Method

Preheat the oven to 180C/350F/gas 4.

Beat the eggs and sugar until light and fluffy. Mix together flour, baking powder, cinnamon and walnuts. Fold this in to the sugar and egg mix.

Peel and core the apples, slice into 0.5 cm slices. Line a 23 cm cake tin with baking paper, put a layer of apple in the bottom, pour the cake mixture on top and lay the rest of the apple on top of that. Sprinkle with ground cinnamon and sugar. Place in the oven for 40-50 minutes, test with a knife; it should come out clean.

To make the crème anglaise, follow the custard recipe on page 148 but leave out the cornflour.

Serve hot with crème anglaise.

Beetroot Fruit Cake with Lemon Icing

Sara adores beetroot so it often appears on our menus. Beetroot, unlike carrot, is rarely used as a pudding though despite its sweet taste and wonderful rich colour.

Ingredients *(serves 6)*

- ~ 250 g butter
- ~ 250 g caster sugar
- ~ Zest of 1 lemon
- ~ 2 eggs
- ~ 150 g plain flour
- ~ 150 g self raising flour
- ~ 1 tsp baking powder
- ~ 150 g dried fruit (raisins, currants and apricots but you could add any dried fruit)
- ~ 250 g raw grated beetroot
- ~ 200 g icing sugar, sieved
- ~ Juice of 1 lemon
- ~ 200 ml double cream

Method

Preheat the oven to 180C/350F/gas 4.

Cream the butter, sugar and lemon zest with an electric or hand whisk, until it's white in colour. Drop in one egg at a time, whisking slowly.

Sieve flours and baking powder, and then fold into the mix adding the dried fruit and beetroot.

Butter a 20 cm long, 7 cm deep loaf tin, line with baking paper, and fill with the mixture. Put in the oven and bake for 45 minutes. To test it's cooked insert a knife in the centre, it should come out clean. When it's ready, turn out of the tin onto a

cooling rack for half an hour. Place the cake on a serving plate.

Mix the sieved icing sugar and lemon juice with a hand whisk then add cream and whisk till it reaches the consistency of whipped cream. It should peak when you pull a spoon out. Then chill in the fridge for 15 minutes.

Spread icing on top of cake or place in a piping bag (this can be improvised with baking paper) and pipe on. Finish with dusting of icing sugar and serve.

Paulo Aquino (Head kitchen porter) & Ntim Kwadwo (Kitchen porter & waiter)

Bread

Crispy Bread (Knäckebröd)
Large White Brioche Loaf
Ntim's Bread – Classic Loaf
Mixed Flour & Seed Bread
Foccacia
Sourdough Rye

Crispy Bread (Knäckebröd)

This is one of Sara's Swedish recipes. It will keep for three weeks in an airtight container, complements cheese or pâtés brilliantly and works as a gift wrapped with ribbon!

Ingredients *(makes 30 discs)*
- 25 g dry yeast or 50 g fresh yeast
- 250 ml warm water
- 1 tsp salt
- 2 tsp caraway seeds or fennel seeds
- 2 tsp golden syrup or honey
- 2 tbsp olive oil
- 100 g wholemeal flour
- 100 g oats
- 300 g plain flour (keep some for dusting the table)

Method
Heat the oven to 220C/425F/gas 7.

Dissolve the yeast in the warm water, add salt, the seeds, golden syrup and oil, and mix well. Add the flours and oats and knead for 5 minutes. If the dough is too wet, add some more plain flour. Continue kneading at least until the dough no longer sticks to the bowl.

Leave to rise in the bowl in a warm place, covered with a clean tea towel for 20 minutes.

Grease a baking tray, or line with baking paper; knead the dough on a floured surface. Divide into 30 balls and roll them out as thinly as you can (less than 5 mm if possible) and prick with a fork. Using a circular pastry cutter, cut a 2.5 cm hole in the middle of each disk. Place bread disks on the baking tray in the oven. Bake for about 15 minutes, or until crispy. Remove the discs and transfer to a wire rack. (The discs can be rolled out slightly thicker before baking and eaten as bread instead.)

Large White Brioche Loaf

This is a brioche-style loaf. I think it's best eaten hot, fresh from the oven, with lots of butter or with jam but it makes a wonderful breakfast toast too. Use leftovers for summer pudding or bread and butter pudding.

Ingredients *(makes 1 loaf)*
- 250 ml warm milk
- 2 tsp honey
- 2 tsp dried yeast
- 500-600 g bread flour
- 1 tsp salt
- 1 egg, beaten
- 50 g butter, melted

Method
Place the milk and honey in a saucepan and heat it to about body temperature. Put the yeast in a jug and pour the milk over it, dissolving thoroughly with a wooden spoon.

Put 500 g of flour and the salt in a large mixing bowl. Add the yeast mix, beaten egg and melted butter. Mix thoroughly. You might need to add more flour to get it to a dough. Knead for about 10 minutes. You are looking for a smooth ball that leaves the sides of the bowl. Cover with a tea towel and leave to rise for 30 minutes. It should double in size and be soft like a baby's bottom!

Grease a 28 cm bread tin. Punch down the dough, dust the table with flour and knead the bread for 5 minutes. Shape the dough by folding so it fits the shape of the bread tin. Place in the tin with the fold on the bottom. Cover and leave to rise for 30 minutes.

Pre-heat the oven to 200C/400F/gas 6. Bake bread in the oven for 30 minutes till it's browning on top. Tap the bottom of the loaf, listen for a hollow sound to check it's cooked. Allow to cool.

Ntim's Bread – Classic Loaf

Ntim has been working as a kitchen porter, waiter and comis chef at the Duke for over 5 years. He bakes our bread in the mornings along with Paulo. They both knock up a fine loaf, and this is Ntim's perfected recipe. Add seeds, nuts or a good cheddar for variations on the loaf.

Ingredients *(makes 1 loaf)*

- 3 tsp dried yeast
- 1 tsp honey or malt syrup
- 1 tsp olive oil
- 600 ml warm water, body temperature
- 500 g white flour
- 500 g brown flour
- 1 tsp salt

Method

Put the yeast, honey or malt syrup, olive oil and water in a bowl. Stir with a wooden spoon, cover with a clean tea towel and let sit in a warm place for an hour.

After 10 minutes, check to see the yeast is creating foam on top, if this hasn't happened, discard and try again.

In a large bowl mix the flours and the salt. Add the yeast mix to the flour. Mix in thoroughly with your hands, making a smooth dough that cleans the sides of the bowl. Leave to stand for an hour in a warm place.

Punch the dough down and knead for 5 minutes. Shape into 2 round loaves by folding, or if you prefer, into buns. Place on a floured baking tray, cover and leave to rise for 30 minutes or until it has doubled in size.

Pre-heat the oven to 200C/400F/gas 6.

Lightly sprinkle some water on top, and bake in the oven for about 30 minutes, till it browns and when you tap the bottom it sounds hollow. Allow to cool on a cooling rack.

Mixed Flour & Seed Bread

A deliciously healthy bread. You can vary the flours to what you have available. You can also add other nuts and seeds like walnuts, hazelnuts or pumpkin seeds.

Ingredients *(makes 2 small loaves)*
- 400 ml warm water
- 3 tsp dried yeast or double the amount of fresh
- 2 tsp honey
- 1 tbsp olive oil
- 200 g spelt flour
- 120 g rye flour
- 100 g wholewheat bread flour
- 100 g white bread flour
- 10 g linseeds
- 50 g sesame seeds
- 50 g sunflower seeds

Method

Dissolve the yeast, honey, and olive oil in a bowl with the warm water. Leave for 10 minutes in a warm place. If you don't get a nice froth on top after that, discard and start again.

Place the flours and seeds in a large mixing bowl, stir together, and then add the yeast mix. With your hands, mix together. If the mix is too wet, slowly add more bread flour. Knead for about 5 minutes. Your dough should be soft, not too sticky, but able to clean off the bowl. Leave for an hour in a warm place to rise, or until the dough has doubled in size.

Preheat the oven to 200C/400F/gas 6.

Punch the dough down and divide into two. Shape into 2 fat sausages.

Dust a large baking tray with flour, place your loaves onto it and leave to rise for a further half hour or until the size has doubled. Bake in the oven for 30 minutes.

Test to see if it's cooked by tapping the bottom of the bread, it should sound hollow, like knocking on a door. Allow to cool on a cooling rack.

Foccacia

This Italian bread is almost a meal in itself. Serve it hot, with olive oil to dip into. You can add any herbs you want to the bread, try marjoram, thyme or sage, also olives, sundried tomatoes, chillies, cheese or peppers.

Ingredients *(makes 1 tray, serves 6)*
- 450 ml warm water
- 2 tsp dried yeast
- 1 tsp honey
- 2 tbsp olive oil
- 700-800 g bread flour
- 2 tsp salt
- 1 tsp Malden sea salt
- 2 cloves garlic, finely chopped
- 1 sprig rosemary, chopped
- 2 tbsp olive oil

Method

Put the water, yeast, honey, olive oil, and half the flour in a bowl. Mix with a wooden spoon until smooth. Cover and leave for 30 minutes.

Mix in the rest of the flour and the 2 teaspoons of salt, knead for about 5 minutes adding more flour if it's too runny, it should leave the sides of the bowl. Cover with a tea towel and allow to stand for a further 30 minutes.

Preheat the oven to 220C/425F/gas 7.

Lightly oil a 20 x 30 x 5 cm baking tray. Put the dough into the baking tray and ease it into the corners with your finger tips.

Punch your fingers into the dough, making indents with your finger tips, creating a consistent lumpy pattern across the top of the bread. Cover with a tea towel and leave to stand for 30 minutes.

Punch the dough again with your finger tips. Sprinkle the dough with sea salt, rosemary, garlic and olive oil. Place in the oven for about 30 minutes. It should be nice and golden brown when you take it out. Allow to cool on a rack before cutting up.

Sourdough Rye

Sourdough is a rich and tasty bread which is produced all over the world. Starters are even handed down through families in some cultures. Our starter at the Duke of Cambridge came from John Lister and Clive Mellum at Shipton Mill; theirs is about 30 years old.

Sourdough starters have a bit of mystique about them, with people thinking they are impossible to begin and maintain. They are precious, but they are not hard to get going at all and extremely easy to manage. You will have created a living product, so it does require some care and attention. If you are going to be a regular baker, you must keep your starter in a coolish place and feed daily. As you remove some for cooking, you feed it again with flour and water. The quantities don't matter that much, take what we have written here as a guide for the daily feeding, but you will find your own way.

Brown or rye flour will work best for a feed as it has the most natural yeast in, but white is possible, just slower. Good quality organic flour is essential though. For less regular baking, keep it in the fridge, it will last a week or 2 without feeding. When you plan to bake you will need to remove it from the fridge 24 hours before use and feed. It will also benefit from a good beating every now and then, whisk it with a fork or whisk, for 3 or 4 minutes.

With this starter, feed for a couple of weeks (discarding what you are not using if you are not baking with it) to get it to a really healthy state. It will smell sour, but it can also smell alcoholic, cheesy, bitter or bread like. Then you can keep it in the fridge if you wish. You can now give tubs of your starter to friends to use.

Ingredients – Starter
- 100 g rye flour
- 125 ml warm water

Method
1st day: Mix the starter ingredients together in a tupperware dish or something with a lid. Whisk thoroughly getting in lots of air. Cover with a wet tea towel if you are using a bowl, not clingfilm. Leave for 24 hours. Keep the starter in a warm place for the first 2 days, somewhere like an airing cupboard or warm kitchen.

2nd day: Feed, mix in the same ingredients starting with the warm water and thoroughly whisking in the flour – leave for 24 hours.

3rd day: Repeat but with cold water. Find a coolish place to store your starter. It will need a permanent home if you are going to continue using it. If it's too warm it will be too lively and you may kill it.

4th day: Bake the bread using the starter.

Ingredients – Dough
- 350 ml warm water
- 150 g rye flour
- 2 large serving spoons of sourdough starter
- 450 g bread flour
- 1 tsp salt

Method
Put the warm water in a mixing bowl and add 150 g of the starter, mix in. Add to this the 150 g of rye flour and 150 g of the bread flour and stir with a wooden spoon until you have a runny dough. Cover and let stand in a warm place for 6-12 hours or do this stage last thing at night and come back to it in the morning.

Add the remaining 300 g of bread flour and the teaspoon of salt to the runny mix. Knead the loaf for at least 5 minutes. Leave in a warm place for an hour or so.

Knead again for a further 5 minutes and leave for another hour. Repeat once more and then shape into a long or round loaf. Cover with a tea towel and leave in a warm place for 1-4 hours, until it has doubled in size.

Preheat the oven to 220C/425F/gas 7.

Bake in the oven, on a floured baking tray, for 10 minutes at the high setting, making sure it doesn't brown too much, then reduce the oven temperature to 180C/350F/gas 4 for a further 40 minutes or until the bread is hollow sounding when tapped on the bottom.

The baking process will benefit from water in the oven, so either pour half a cup of water into the bottom of the oven immediately before placing your loaves in, or put half a cup in a baking tray at the bottom of the oven.

The bread will also benefit from a hot baking tray, so you can preheat a tray and transfer your bread onto it. But it can all seem like too much work, so only if you really fancy a time of it!